Women of Twilight

An all-women play

by Sylvia Rayman

SERVING THEATRE

S F

SINCE 1830

WWW.SAMUELFRENCH.CO.UK
WWW.SAMUELFRENCH.COM

ISBN 978-0-573-11245-4

www.samuelfrench.co.uk
www.samuelfrench.com

FOR AMATEUR PRODUCTION ENQUIRIES

UNITED KINGDOM AND WORLD
EXCLUDING NORTH AMERICA

plays@SamuelFrench-London.co.uk

020 7255 4302/01

Each title is subject to availability from Samuel French, depending upon country of performance.

WOMEN OF TWILIGHT

Women of Twilight

First produced at the Regent Theatre, Hayes, under the direction of JEAN SHEPEARD, on 30th July, 1951, with the following cast of characters:—

HELEN ALLISTAIR	Beatrix Mackay
CHRISTINE RALSTON	Delphine Muir
JESS	Ana Glyn
ROSIE	Ann Purkiss
LAURA	Ann Jellicoe
VIVIANNE	Shelley Lynn
VERONICA	Maureen Hurley
OLGA	Olga Lowe
SAL	Lynda King
MOLLY	Mary Neelands
NURSE	Evelyn Dysart

Produced by RONA LAURIE

and subsequently produced at the Embassy, Vaudeville and Victoria Palace Theatres, London.

The action of the play takes place in the semi-basement living-room of a house near London.

SCENES

ACT I
Scene 1. Evening.
Scene 2. A few weeks later.

ACT II
Scene 1. Morning, one month later.
Scene 2. Two months later.

ACT III
Scene 1. Four days later.
Scene 2. Three days later.

TIME: the present.

No reference in this play is intended to any person alive or dead.

NOTE: *Running time, excluding intervals, is approximately two hours.*

PRODUCER'S NOTE

THIS is a strong, forceful play calling for great sincerity both in production and acting. It has suspense and tension, and is full of effective situations. Perhaps the play's greatest strength is in its dialogue, which is colloquial and racy. The characters are clear-cut and vividly drawn, giving unusual acting opportunities.

Although the play deals with a social evil of our time, urging greater humanity to the unmarried mother, this theme is woven into the texture of the drama and never becomes mere propaganda. The situations are strong, the language sometimes crude, but this strength and crudeness heighten the moral effect of the play as it challenges the social conscience of the audience.

When the play was originally produced at Hayes, we went all out for sincerity. The play must be produced as it is written and there must be no straining after comic effect; that is—the comedy must be played straight. Allow it to arise naturally out of the dialogue. The characters must never be allowed to indulge in self-pity, and mere sentimentality must be avoided likewise. It is important to find the right relationship between the various characters, and one of the linchpins of the play is the tender, unsentimental friendship between Christine and Vivianne.

The fact that so many of the girls have emotional breakdowns on the stage presents a problem. If they are all allowed to break down in the same way it will become monotonous. There is all the difference in the world between Vivianne's agonised sobbing, at the end of Act II—Scene 1, and Veronica's disillusioned tears in the following scene. Without some distinction the result will tend to be a monotonous obbligato of noisy, hysterical emotion. The end of Act III—Scene 1, requires particularly careful handling. Much depends on the tact with which the actress playing Vivianne handles the scene: she should strike a balance between a too painful realism and stage convention.

The next point is a purely technical one. However sincerely WOMEN OF TWILIGHT is played, it will be found impossible to sustain the tension unless the production has pace. This will make the occasional, dramatic pauses far more telling. A good example of this can be found in the breakfast scene at the beginning of Act II. If the pace be kept up until Christine's line, " It's to-day they're hanging Johnny Stanton ", the pause that follows is doubly effective, and the charged atmosphere of the rest of the scene gains enormously by altered tempo.

The four main characters are Vivianne, Helen, Jess and Christine, and the whole balance of the play depends on their relationship to each other being right. Whenever Vivianne comes into the room the atmosphere is heightened, not only as a result of what she says and does, but by virtue of her dramatic personality: she alternates between world-weariness and a kind of gay defiance.

Christine is a thoroughly sane and healthy girl. We know that her present situation is only a passing phase, and that she will come out of it unscathed. She is able to help Vivianne by her strength and cheerful vitality: qualities which are, incidentally, of great value in lifting the play, especially in her entrance in Act II—Scene 2.

Helen is a subtly-written character, capable of more than one interpretation. A great deal of her apparent callousness can be explained if we remember that she thinks of herself as a " lady ", and has an almost Victorian disregard for the poor. She sees the sickliness of Rosie's baby dispassionately, as the result of generations of squalor, of ignorance and unwholesome stock. At times she seems genuinely fond of Vivianne and anxious to help her. Helen is restless and highly-strung, and it will help the actress playing her if she is given a good deal of stage " business " to do. We should get the feeling, during the play, that a net is slowly closing round her.

Jess is a buxom cockney, combining coarse humour and animal vitality with a streak of cruelty. This is seen in the way she taunts Vivianne about Johnny. She stays with Helen just as long as it suits her, but when Helen turns to her in real trouble she has no hesitation in walking out on her. The actress playing Jess must be able to let herself go. There is a great deal of comedy in her part but she must be careful not to overplay it.

Rosie is a little cockney factory-girl, tawdrily smart. She has a perky vitality and, when she is distressed about her baby, great pathos.

Laura is about forty, and looks like an efficient secretary. She should wear a neat, dark suit, speak in a low, controlled voice and move briskly and definitely.

Olga and Veronica are excellent foils for each other: Olga, a warm-hearted cockney with a good sense of humour, and Veronica, a pretty suburban girl defiantly trying to keep up tennis-club standards in her present nightmare surroundings. It is only when she breaks down to Vivianne that we see her real unhappiness and bewilderment. This is a most interesting part with a beautifully-written emotional scene.

The actress playing Sal must bring great sensitivity to her reading of the part. It may help her to use a slight hesitancy of speech. Her movements should be awkward and her laboured processes of thought obvious to the audience. She speaks slowly, with a rough accent, but she must be careful to vary the tempo in her long scene with Vivianne.

Molly is a good-natured Irish girl, not at all abashed by her present situation, and the Nurse brings a certain astringent quality to the play. The latter part can be played with a Scotch accent but this is not essential. She must be brisk and efficient, with a good sense of humour, and she must be able to stand up to Helen and Jess.

When presenting WOMEN OF TWILIGHT a small stage is no disadvantage; in fact, a slightly cramped set helps the atmosphere.

RONA LAURIE

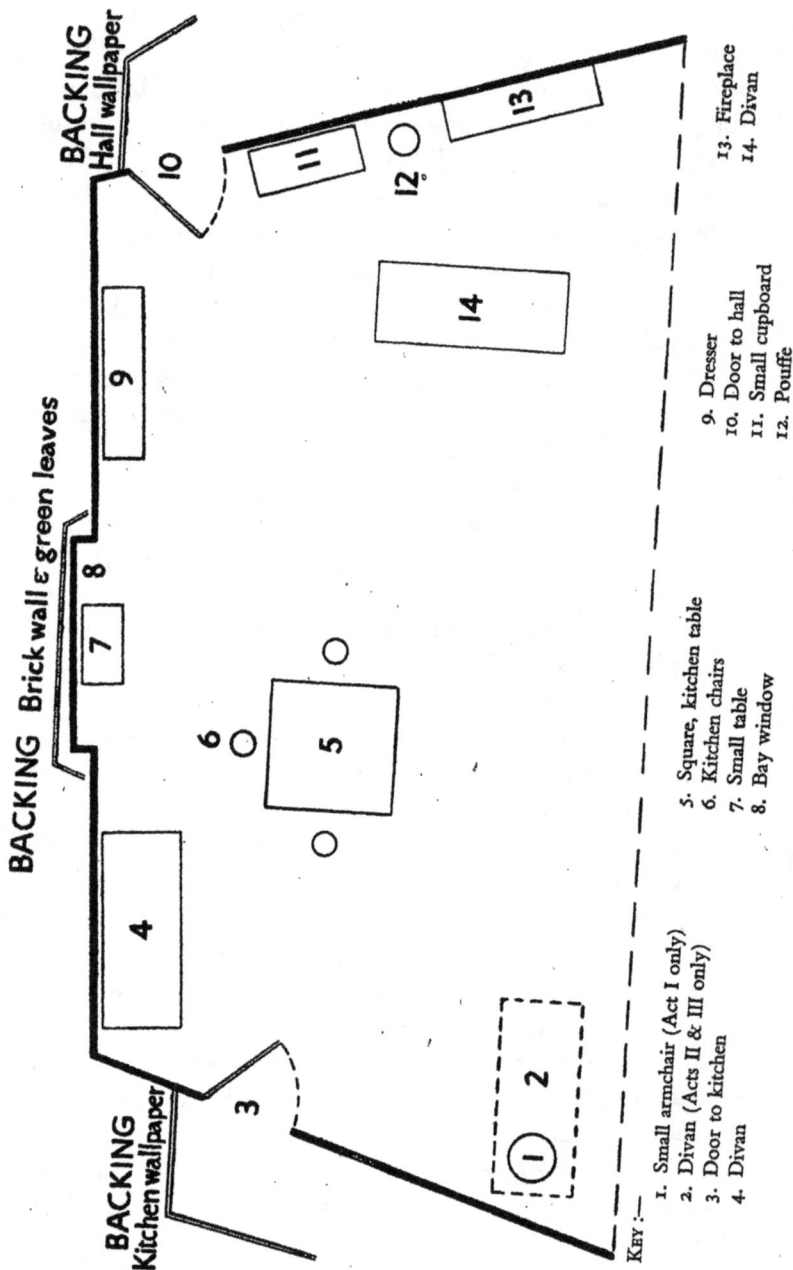

BACKING Brick wall & green leaves

BACKING Hall wallpaper

BACKING Kitchen wallpaper

KEY :—

1. Small armchair (Act I only)
2. Divan (Acts II & III only)
3. Door to kitchen
4. Divan

5. Square, kitchen table
6. Kitchen chairs
7. Small table
8. Bay window

9. Dresser
10. Door to hall
11. Small cupboard
12. Pouffe

13. Fireplace
14. Divan

WOMEN OF TWILIGHT

ACT I

SCENE I

A semi-basement living-room in a house near London. The wall-paper is dingy, the carpet threadbare. There is a small kitchen table up C. *with three plain chairs; a divan against the wall up* R., *another down* L. *in front of the fireplace. A dresser stands above the door leading to the hall* L. *The general effect is one of untidiness and neglect. In front of the fire is a small clothes-horse with baby clothes. An improvised clothes line stretches across the dresser top. Shabby curtains are drawn back from the bay-window up* C. *showing shabbier lace curtains and the dusk beyond.*

      HELEN *and* CHRISTINE *are standing* L. *and* R.C. CHRISTINE *has a baby in her arms.*

HELEN. You'd better let me take him now. I expect you're ready for a rest.

CHRISTINE. Shouldn't I bath him and put him to bed?

HELEN. No, I'll do that to-night, you've had a tiring day; besides if you are going to be out at work he'll have to get used to being cared for by strangers.

CHRISTINE. He's always been cared for by strangers. He's hardly been with me at all. (*She hands baby over to* HELEN.)

HELEN. That's not surprising, is it, since he's only three weeks old? The girls will be in for their tea any moment; just sit down and make yourself at home. (*She sits on divan* L.)

CHRISTINE. Couldn't I come with you?

HELEN. I wouldn't just at present; I want to get the other children off to bed. Most of the mothers are out all day, so you can imagine I have my hands full.

CHRISTINE. How many are there?

HELEN. Babies or mothers? I've got four girls at the moment, but I'm expecting two new arrivals in the next few days. There are ten babies, counting those mothers who don't live on the premises.

CHRISTINE. You don't know what a relief it's been to me, finding a place where there's no objection to children.

HELEN. Objection! This house is open to children first and foremost.

CHRISTINE. I used to have a flat in Kensington but as soon as my landlady heard about the baby she gave notice to quit, and they wouldn't let me leave the hospital with him unless I had a place to go.

HELEN. Most young mothers want to keep their children, but it wouldn't do to have them wandering about the streets. That's why, with a house like this all to myself, I feel that the least I can do is to offer them temporary shelter. I wish I could afford to do it for nothing, but my husband left me very little; as it is, I keep the rents as low as possible.

CHRISTINE. You're very kind.

HELEN. Not at all. I had a child myself once. Well, this won't get the work done. It's time this young man was in bed. (*She rises and goes to door up* L.)

CHRISTINE. You're sure there's nothing I can do?
                (*The clock in the hall strikes six.*)

HELEN. Not on your first day here. We usually take it in turns to get the tea. Sit down and relax.

        (CHRISTINE *looks about doubtfully, picks up her case from chair* R. *of table, then puts it down again.* JESSIE *enters* D.R. *She is a big, buxom, blonde girl with a strong cockney accent.*)

JESSIE. Why the 'ell don't you put the light on?

CHRISTINE. I'm sorry, I couldn't find the switch.

JESSIE. Eh? Oh, I didn't realise we 'ad company.

CHRISTINE. I'm not company exactly—I've come to live here. (*She moves down* C. *looking around the room—which is less inviting in the harsh light. She sees for the first time the shabby condition of the furniture, the dust on the carpet, the pile of dirty crockery on the table.*)

JESSIE. Nellie know you're 'ere?

CHRISTINE (*starting*). Who?

JESSIE. Nellie—Mrs. Allistair—does she know you've come?

CHRISTINE. Oh yes! She's just gone up to put my son to bed.

JESSIE (*knowingly*). Ah! Well, seeing as you're one of us you'd better not stand on ceremony. (*Moves to table.*) Sit yourself.
> (CHRISTINE *does not answer—she is still surveying the room with distaste.* JESSIE *laughs loudly, getting cups together.*) What did you expect—the Ritz?

CHRISTINE (*dazedly*). No I—I—maybe you would show me where my room is. If you don't mind, I'd like to unpack.

JESSIE. Your room? This is your room, dear.

CHRISTINE. What do you mean?

JESSIE (*patting the divan bed in the corner up* R.). This is where you're going to sleep—not a bad bed either—Nellie 'ad it upholstered last November.

CHRISTINE. Oh no—I couldn't. (*She moves below table.*)

JESSIE. Couldn't what?

CHRISTINE. Sleep down here! I've paid full board and lodging.

JESSIE. Well there's your lodgin', dear—you should 'ave tried to sleep on it before—springs all coming through and no feathers.

CHRISTINE. There must be some mistake. Mrs. Allistair never told me——

JESSIE. Mrs. Allistair never told anyone nothin'—you've got to find out. You 'adn't an 'ome, 'ad you? You wanted a place to kip?

CHRISTINE. But I wouldn't have considered paying three guineas a week to sleep in somebody's living-room.

JESSIE. You're not paying for the room, duck—you're paying for to keep your kid. No one's going to let their rooms to folks with babies these days—not unless they're bloody millionaires. Maybe you can afford to pay five hundred premium. (*Picking up cups.*)

CHRISTINE. No—no, I can't.

JESSIE. You married?

CHRISTINE (*quickly*). Yes.

JESSIE. Husband walked out on you?

CHRISTINE. No—he's in America—on business. (*She moves* L.)

JESSIE (*turns to her*). No kiddin'? Well—if you're married what are you doing in a joint like this?

CHRISTINE. The reason you've just mentioned—with a small child it's impossible to get a flat. I only left the hospital to-day; someone gave me Mrs. Allistair's address, but I'm afraid she rather misled me.

JESSIE. Well, since you're 'ere you better make yourself at 'ome. Expect you're ready for a cup of tea?

CHRISTINE (*weakly*). Thanks.

(*Exit* JESSIE R. *re-entering almost at once.*)

JESSIE (*looking at her*). It's not so bad, you know—I been 'ere nearly four years.

CHRISTINE. Four years! (*She sits in chair* L. *of table.*)

JESSIE. My youngest's three and an 'alf. Got three more at 'ome with my Mam, so no-one can say I 'aven't done me share. What's yours—a boy? (*She draws heavy curtains.*)

CHRISTINE. Yes. You've really been here as long as that—four years?

JESSIE. Well you got to kip somewhere—and Nellie's not so bad when you get used to 'er; free board and keep for me and the kid in exchange for a bit of plain cooking and a flick around with the duster. (*She comes down* R. *of table.*)

CHRISTINE. I suppose you help her with the children?

JESSIE. No, Sal does most of that. She used to be Nellie's maid before 'er old man died. (*Tapping her forehead.*) She's all right, old Sal, but a little bit lackin' in the upper story.

(*We hear* ROSIE *chatting in hall.*)

CHRISTINE. Do—people usually stay here long?

JESSIE (*sitting in chair* R. *of table*). They come and go—depends on how quickly they can get away. Some of 'em stop a month—some six. They're comin' and goin' all the time.

(JESSIE *breaks off as* ROSIE *and* LAURA *enter.* ROSIE *is a whiny little factory girl of about eighteen;* LAURA *a quiet, neat woman of nearly forty. They both regard* CHRISTINE *with curiosity.*)

JESSIE. Hullo, kids! 'ere's another come to join the 'appy family. Meet Rosie and Laura. I don't believe you told me what your name was.

CHRISTINE (*rising*). Christine—Christine Ralston.

ROSIE (*in a rasping little cockney voice*). Are you stoppin' 'ere?

CHRISTINE. Only until I can fix up somewhere else.

ROSIE (*to* JESSIE). Is she a friend of Nellie Allistair's?

JESSIE. No, she's just the same as all the rest—except she's got a husband in America. (*To* CHRISTINE.) Funny that you heard about this place. Most of the girls is sent down from the 'omes or the convent—but *you* wouldn't have been in touch with anywhere like that?

CHRISTINE (*very uncertain*). I—well—I had to ask advice because I wanted somewhere to leave the baby while I'm out at work.

JESSIE. Don't your 'usband support you?

CHRISTINE. Yes—of course—but we're both young and we'll need a little extra money now we've got a family. It's just till he gets back.

ROSIE. It ain't none of our business. (*She crosses to fireplace, looks in mirror above mantelpiece.*)

LAURA. No, I should think not. (*To* CHRISTINE.) I hope you'll be fairly comfortable. Will you excuse me while I say good-night to my little girl? It's the only time I get a chance to see her.

CHRISTINE. Of course. (*She sits on divan* L.)

(*Exit* LAURA L.)

JESSIE. She's a queer fish. To look at 'er you'd think she was a school marm, *and* to 'ear 'er talk, but she walked in 'ere as bold as brass one day with a little bundle in 'er arms and says to Nellie, " I'm an unmarried mother ".

(*She and* ROSIE *laugh.*)

What gets me is, 'er boy friend would 'ave married 'er but she wasn't 'avin' any. " I don't want no man tied to me," she says, " all I wants is my baby."

ROSIE. If you saw the fuss she makes, you'd think it was the only one alive.

JESSIE. Can you beat it, though? That was all she wanted—went and got herself in the cart on purpose.

ROSIE. Is supper ready, Jess? (*She crosses and sits on divan* R.)

JESSIE. Give me time. It's only 'alf past six.

ROSIE. I'm 'ungry.

JESSIE. You'll 'ave to wait.

CHRISTINE. Is there anywhere I can wash my hands?

JESSIE. Wash your 'ands? Oh, Rosie'll show you—it's just at the top of the stairs,

(*As* CHRISTINE *looks at her hands doubtfully.*)

but if you really want to wash you can do that in the kitchen sink. Nellie don't let us use the bathroom. (*To* ROSIE.) Hey, kid—do you know your Alfie's got another tooth?

ROSIE (*rising—eagerly*). No kiddin'.

JESSIE. Yes—a whopper. (*Moving to* R.) I'd better put them kippers on.

ROSIE. I must go and 'ave a look.

(*Exit* L., *passing* VIVIANNE *as she enters. She does not apologise, but draws away perceptibly with a look of disgust.* VIVIANNE *is about twenty-six. At a glance she appears older for, although very nearly beautiful, she looks worn and haggard. Her clothes are smart and she is defiantly made up, but there is something jaded about her general appearance. She enters like a sleepwalker, blinking a little at the light.* JESSIE *throws her a hostile glance and goes out abruptly to* R. CHRISTINE *glances, puzzled, from one to the other, but* VIVIANNE *does not seem to notice her. She crosses to the divan and with slow, tired movements removes her hat and coat. She throws them down on the divan beside* CHRISTINE.)

CHRISTINE. I'm sorry. Am I sitting on your bed?

VIVIANNE (*with a shrug*). It doesn't matter.

(CHRISTINE *rises and sits on pouffe near fireplace.*)

CHRISTINE (*desperately after an uncomfortable pause*). It's colder now, isn't it? The sun's been lovely all day but now it's getting chilly.

VIVIANNE. Is it? (*Lights a cigarette and lies on divan kicking off her shoes.*)

(LAURA *re-enters* L. *She has taken off her outdoor clothes. Crosses to divan* R. *and sits on the end, takes out knitting from knitting bag.*)

LAURA. What a mess this place is; you can never see the fire for washing.

CHRISTINE. I'm afraid it's rather different from what I expected.

LAURA. One gets used to almost anything. I'm only staying until I find a flat—but you know what that's like nowadays.

CHRISTINE. Yes.

LAURA. Haven't you any family?

CHRISTINE. Only my mother, and she's living with relations.

LAURA. My one idea is to get away before Barbara's old enough to notice her surroundings. That's my little girl you know—she's almost two.

CHRISTINE. You've been here all the time?

LAURA. Since she was six months. The friends I was staying with were leaving the country and all the welfare centres were full up.

(JESSIE *enters from* R.)

JESSIE (*to* CHRISTINE). Can you eat kippers, dear?

CHRISTINE. Yes—thank you.

JESSIE (*to* VIVIANNE). Shall we be having the pleasure of your company at supper?

VIVIANNE. I don't want anything.

JESSIE. Fine—now I'm beginning to get my appetite back.

LAURA (*warningly*). Jess!

JESSIE. I'm not fussy about the company I keep but there's some people that I draw the line at. (*After a pause—to* VIVIANNE.) Was you at the Court to-day?

(VIVIANNE *looks at her but does not answer.*)

I saw in the paper that they 'ad to call out extra police to stop the crowd from breaking in and tearing 'im to pieces.

(ROSIE *enters* L. *and goes to table.*)

LAURA (*worriedly*). Now stop it!

JESSIE. I'd 'ave let 'em string 'im up. It's a waste of time and money giving a man like that a trial. Everyone knows 'e's guilty—why not 'ang 'im and be done with it? (*To* CHRISTINE *—indicating* VIVIANNE.) You know who this is, don't you? She's Johnny Stanton's piece.

CHRISTINE. I've never heard of Johnny Stanton.

JESSIE. Don't you read the papers? Lousy little coward walks into a cinema with a scarf round 'is mouth and a gun in 'is 'and and shoots down three innocent people—all for the sake of a few measly quid—which 'e'd 'oped to spend on 'er, no doubt.

VIVIANNE (*sitting up*). Shut up.

ROSIE. Yes, turn it in, Jess.

JESSIE. 'anging's too good for 'im.

VIVIANNE. I told you to shut up.

JESSIE. It's a free country, ain't it? I've a right to speak me mind.

LAURA. There's no point in keeping on about it, Jess. The law will see that the man's punished.

JESSIE. Yes, but will the law stop 'er from bringing 'is bastard into the world—?

(*Breaks off with a shriek as* VIVIANNE *makes a rush at her.* LAURA *and* CHRISTINE *rise, and* ROSIE *grabs at* JESSIE'S *arm. There is a short struggle.* JESSIE *lets out a scream, clutching her wrist.*)

JESSIE. She scratched me, the little bitch? Can't even fight fair. Look—it could give me blood poisoning.

VIVIANNE. It serves you right. You asked for it, didn't you?
  (ROSIE *and* LAURA *intervene as* JESSIE *attempts to continue*
  the fight. HELEN *enters, crosses swiftly between them* C.)
HELEN. What are you girls thinking of? This is a nice way to
  behave in front of a newcomer, isn't it?
  (JESSIE *mutters.*)
Stop it this instant or you'll both get out. I've told you I will
  not have this brawling in my house.
JESSIE. She started it—scratched me she did.
HELEN. Go back to the kitchen and finish the supper.
  (JESSIE *and* ROSIE *mutter.* LAURA *sits on divan* R. *and*
  resumes her knitting.)
Go on now, at once.
  (JESSIE *remains cursing and muttering, holding her wrists.*)
Vivianne, you look ill: I think you'd better sit down.
VIVIANNE. I'm going out again.
HELEN. Without your supper—don't be silly! All right, Jess,
  and remember what I said. If you can't control your temper
  you will have to go. (*To* VIVIANNE.) That goes for you as
  well.
JESSIE. She started it.
HELEN. I don't care who began it, but I won't have everyone
  else upset because you choose to behave like a couple of
  savages.
JESSIE. It's not fair to expect decent people to live under the
  same roof as 'er. Look what she's done to my wrist.
VIVIANNE. I don't interfere with you. Why can't you leave me
  alone?
HELEN. I'm only interested in maintaining a friendly atmosphere for the benefit of all concerned. (*After a pause.*) I think
  there is something burning in the kitchen—you'd better go
  and see what it is.
  (*Exit* JESSIE *sullenly* R. VIVIANNE *sits down on the divan.*)
  (*As* CHRISTINE *looks uncertainly towards* VIVIANNE.) Now have
  you girls introduced yourselves to Christine?
  W.T.—B

ROSIE. We didn't think she'd want to be introduced to 'er.

HELEN. That'll do, Rosie.

ROSIE. If you don't mind, I think I'll stop in the kitchen where the company's more select.

(*Exit* R.)

HELEN. I'm afraid we're all conspiring to give you a very bad impression. We have our ups and downs like everybody else but usually we're quite a happy household.

CHRISTINE (*dubiously*). Yes—I'm sure. (*After a pause—rapidly.*) Mrs. Allistair, it seems there's some misunderstanding: I was under the impression I should have my own room. (*She crosses to* HELEN C.)

HELEN. My dear, the house is overflowing. I gave up two rooms to the children and I only keep the ground floor for myself. That leaves two bedrooms and a very small box room where the maid sleeps.

CHRISTINE. But you never told me that.

HELEN. I naturally assumed that, as you needed a place so desperately . . .

CHRISTINE (*interrupting*). I've never shared a bedroom in my life before. Where shall I keep my belongings? I shan't have any privacy.

HELEN. I'm really very sorry. I wish I could do better, but I've nothing else to offer at the moment. Laura's room-mate will be arriving some time next week, and Jess and Rosie are together. Where else *can* I put you?

CHRIS (*desperately*). I wouldn't mind if it were a box room or an attic.

HELEN. Well, if you make the best of it for now, I'll have a little talk to Sal. Perhaps we could squeeze her into a corner of the nursery. Anyway, I'll have to think about it.

LAURA (*moving* C. *to* HELEN). Mrs. Allistair—I was going to ask you—did Barbara have a bath before she went to bed to-night? I noticed just now her little hands were quite grubby.

(CHRISTINE *crosses to table.*)

HELEN (*sharply*). I naturally assume she had a bath. Getting the children ready for bed is one of Sally's duties. I can't be everywhere at once.

LAURA. At the price I pay here, it's reasonable to expect she gets proper attention.

HELEN. Do you know anyone who'd give you better value for your money? (*As* LAURA *does not reply.*) Very well, then, if you are not satisfied with the attention Barbara's getting, you'd better make arrangements to come home early to attend to her yourself.

LAURA. You know that's quite impossible at the moment.

HELEN. It's also quite impossible for me to supervise everything personally. I do whenever possible, but this evening Christine arrived when we were in the middle of getting the children ready for bed.

LAURA. I just thought I'd mention it.

HELEN. Mention it to Sally, Laura.

LAURA. I certainly will.

JESSIE (*puts her head round the door* R). Come and get it.
(*Exit at once.*)

HELEN. Ah—supper. (*Exit* CHRISTINE R. *To* VIVIANNE.) Aren't you going, Vivianne?

VIVIANNE (*shortly*). No.

HELEN. You ought to eat, you know. You're not being fair to the baby. (*She moves to* VIVIANNE.)

VIVIANNE (*turning away*). Oh, leave me alone!

HELEN. I'll have a private word with Jessie Smithson: she must be made to understand that the law is meting out punishment to the man you used to call your husband and in doing so is punishing you.

VIVIANNE. They haven't found him guilty yet.

HELEN. You might bear in mind that, in spite of these little unpleasantnesses that arise, you are fortunate to have a home at all. Not many people would open their doors to you at the moment.

VIVIANNE (*with a look of hatred*). I realise I'm indebted to you.

HELEN. That's one way of putting it—but I should prefer you to believe I helped you out of kindness.

VIVIANNE. Kindness! Why should you be kind to me?

HELEN. For the same reason I try to be kind to anyone who comes to me in trouble.

VIVIANNE. That's very noble. Now leave me alone.

(*As* HELEN *does not move.*)

Go and leave me—I'm sick of being watched. Don't you think it's bad enough to have people watching me all day?

HELEN. It's only natural, isn't it? What else can you expect when you become implicated in an unsavoury case like this. (*More gently.*) You're going through a very dreadful time, my child. Perhaps you feel you're doing right in standing by the father of your baby—regardless of the fact that he's committed murder.

VIVIANNE (*breaking in sharply*). They haven't proved it.

HELEN. You know they will. You couldn't have lived with him for all those years without discovering what sort of person he was.

VIVIANNE. The papers only print the bad things. They couldn't know what I know.

HELEN. If you take that attitude you can hardly expect to be considered any sort of judge. You stayed with him, even when you discovered your marriage was bigamous. It's not surprising that people like Jess are aggressive towards you. You could win them over easily enough if you admitted you only stayed with him because you were afraid.

VIVIANNE. Afraid of Johnny?

HELEN. Weren't you? Not even when you knew about the murder?

VIVIANNE (*staring at her blandly*). I didn't know. How could I know, before they've proved it?

HELEN. Oh, you're a very stupid, obstinate girl!

(*Breaks off as* CHRISTINE *enters with two cups of tea. We hear laughter and voices from the kitchen.*)

Good night, my dears, and I hope you sleep well; and remember, Vivianne, no more quarrelling.

(*Exit* L.)

CHRISTINE. Good night. (*To* VIVIANNE.) I brought you some tea.

VIVIANNE (*after a pause—taking cup*). Oh—thanks.

CHRISTINE (*takes her cup to pouffe by fireplace*). To tell you the truth, I wanted to get away—I find those girls a little over-whelming. (*As* VIVIANNE *does not answer.*) Is Mrs. Allistair really a philanthropist?

VIVIANNE (*laughs harshly*). What do *you* think? That's right—have a good look. It's a pity I'm so bloody photogenic.

CHRISTINE. I'm sorry, I didn't mean to stare. As a matter of fact I've not been following the case—the only section of the paper I've been reading is the " property to let " column. I've got to find a flat that's big enough for three. My husband's coming home soon.

VIVIANNE. You've got a husband?

CHRISTINE. Hasn't anybody else here?

VIVIANNE. I don't think so—at the moment.

CHRISTINE. He's in America, so of course he hasn't seen our baby yet.

VIVIANNE (*picking up newspaper again*). That'll give him something to look forward to.

CHRISTINE (*suddenly—in a rush*). No, I haven't—it's not true.

VIVIANNE (*wearily—looking at her*). What?

CHRISTINE. I haven't got a husband—we're not married yet. I haven't told the others—only Mrs. Allistair, so don't say anything.

VIVIANNE. They'll find out. They find out everything.

CHRISTINE. We're going to be married as soon as he gets back. You don't believe me, do you?

VIVIANNE (*reading paper*). Of course—it's the easiest thing in in the world to believe.

CHRISTINE. He didn't know about the baby.

VIVIANNE. Convenient for him.

CHRISTINE. Oh no! It's not like that—when I wrote and told him he wanted to come home right away, but I wouldn't let him risk his job. That's why I haven't told the others. We're as good as married, aren't we?

VIVIANNE. Why did you tell me?

CHRISTINE. I don't know. Maybe I just felt like unburdening myself.

VIVIANNE. I hope you're not one of those women who likes to keep letting her hair down—because there's nothing I loathe more than a cosy little chat after the lights are out.

CHRISTINE. I wouldn't dream of imposing on your privacy. Anyway I shan't be staying here long enough for that.

VIVIANNE. You're lucky. (*As* CHRISTINE *is silent and obviously hurt.*) Look, kid—I wasn't being nasty—but it's really better for you not to talk to me.

CHRISTINE. You mean because of what the others will say? I don't care—I'm old enough to form my own opinions.

VIVIANNE. I don't want anyone feeling sorry for me. I spoilt all that by not being sorry for myself. I lived for years with Johnny Stanton, and I'd go back to him to-morrow— whether he was innocent or guilty.

CHRISTINE. You must have loved him very much.

VIVIANNE (*after a pause*). We'd got—used to each other.

CHRISTINE. Does he know about the baby?

VIVIANNE. Hell—what difference does it make whether he knows or doesn't know?

CHRISTINE. How dreadful for you.

VIVIANNE. Oh shut up!

CHRISTINE. I'm sorry—but there's not much I can say.

VIVIANNE. Well, never mind—it couldn't make a lot of difference.

(*Rises and takes cream, towel and hand-mirror from cupboard above fireplace.*)

CHRISTINE. Are you going to bed? What about the others? They'll be coming back in here.

VIVIANNE (*sitting on divan again*). So what? We get wakened up at six when Jess comes down to start the breakfasts.

CHRISTINE. You'll never be able to sleep with everyone talking. (*She crosses to divan* R. *putting her cup down on the table on the way.*)

VIVIANNE (*with a shrug*). Laura never stays up late—she likes to read in bed—and Jess and Rosie stick together. Either they'll get so mad at me that they'll sweep out, or I'll get so mad at them *I'll* sweep out. It's a battle royal that rages every night. (*She starts to remove her make-up.*)

CHRISTINE (*slowly*). I think it's awful.

VIVIANNE. Oh, you'll get used to it. I look at it like this—if Johnny gets off with " life " he'll have to face worse inconveniences. All right—if he's got to take it, I can. And if he dies—well, maybe I'll die too. Lots of women die in childbirth—and the life I'm living isn't going to make it any easier.

CHRISTINE. You shouldn't talk like that.

VIVIANNE (*returns cream etc. to cupboard, then gets night-dress and dressing-gown from under pillow, kicks off her skirt and gets into her dressing-gown*). I didn't want this baby; I'd never have let it go so far, only I was so sick with worry when they arrested Johnny that I just didn't notice what was happening to me. Seems silly, doesn't it? A girl who's supposed to know all the answers! That's where I'm different from the others—most of them who come here are poor little fools who got into a jam and didn't know how to get out of it. Rosie's people sling her out, and her boy friend's under twenty-one and doesn't earn enough to support her; nine out of ten are like Rosie, and they're better game for Allistair than the wiser ones. She takes every penny they've got and lets them live in squalor and talks to them like the Salvation Army. I bet she fooled you, too, with all her saccharine talk about taking the homeless in off the streets and giving them shelter; shelter's just about all at three guineas a week—with a quid on top if you want her to look after your kid.

CHRISTINE. It's—exploitation.

VIVIANNE (*laughs at her shocked expression*). You're not kidding. (*Climbs into bed with a sigh of satisfaction.*) God, I was ready to drop. Come on, Jessie, try and move me now.

    (*Stretches luxuriously.* ROSIE *and* JESSIE *enter from the kitchen.* JESSIE *glares at* VIVIANNE *darkly, but does not speak. She kicks off her shoes and drops on the second divan removing her apron.*)

JESSIE. See if there's any music on the wireless, Rosie.

    (ROSIE *switches on the radio on the dresser. Dance music blares forth. She dances round the room, humming dreamily.*)

ROSIE. My Bert's a smashin' dancer. 'e used to take me to the Palais twice a week before 'e started saving up.

JESSIE (*to* CHRISTINE—*confidentially*). Bert's—'er—Alfie's daddy. They're goin' to get married when 'e's twenty-one.

    (CHRISTINE *nods with polite interest.*)

ROSIE. 'is auntie's goin' to rent us a room in 'er 'ouse.

JESSIE (*with a wink*). That'll be the day.

ROSIE (*centre*). Only a few more weeks, and I can tell old Nellie what to do with 'er bleeding charity.

JESSIE. Hey—there's a lady present.

ROSIE (*twirls around and lands in chair* L. *of table*). A few weeks ain't long.

JESSIE. Nah—a few weeks is nothin'. (*To* CHRISTINE.) Dare say your old man'll be back by then?

CHRISTINE. I certainly hope so.

JESSIE (*nodding at* VIVIANNE). Give you three guesses where 'ers'll be. She'll have to work for 'er livin' then—no more Ritzy flats or fancy jewels to flash around.

(VIVIANNE *covers the bracelet on her wrist. It is an elaborate affair set with quite good stones.*)

JESSIE. It's a wicked shame to bring a child into the world with a start like that.

ROSIE. Oh, don't start again.

VIVIANNE. You keep asking for a row—one of these days you're going to get one. You haven't seen me lose my temper yet—I may have learned to sound my aitches but, you can take it from me, I was brought up in just as tough a school as you were.

JESSIE. Reform school, no doubt. I'm shaking with fear.

(LAURA *enters from kitchen with a plate and dishcloth in her hand.*)

ROSIE. Jessie, aren't we goin' to the pictures?

JESSIE. Thought you were savin' for your trousseau.

ROSIE. Well, everybody's got to 'ave a bit of pleasure sometimes.

LAURA. Isn't it your turn to clean this room?

ROSIE. Go on! I did it last time. What you think I am, slaving away in a factory all day—then comin' home to do the charin'?

LAURA. It's really a disgrace! Jessie didn't do it last night and it got missed the night before, because Sally had one of her turns.

JESSIE. If you're so fussy, why don't you do it yourself?

LAURA. It's not my turn.

JESSIE. Then what are you worryin' about?

LAURA. All that dust and dirt—it's unhygienic.

JESSIE (JESSIE *and* ROSIE *laugh*). Unhygienic! 'ear that, Rosie! Well, ain't that just too bad? It'll 'ave to stay that way. Come on, kid, we'll go and 'ave a bob's worth at the Plaza. Come on.

(*Exeunt* JESSIE *and* ROSIE L. *talking.*)

VIVIANNE (*rising and turning off radio*). Hurry up and get into bed, I'm absolutely dead.

CHRISTINE (*rising*). All right.

VIVIANNE. You'll have to wash in the kitchen, but make it a lick and a promise. We don't often have the chance to get a decent rest in this house. (*Takes sponge bag and towel from cupboard top and goes out R.—calling off.*) Wait a minute, Laura, don't use all the hot water. Oh, damn!

> (*Left alone, CHRISTINE takes her suitcase and opens it on the divan. She takes off her blouse, puts on her dressing-gown, and then slips out of her skirt. Suddenly she sits down and begins to cry silently. VIVIANNE enters R. almost at once. She pauses, watching her—then crosses to behind her, hesitantly; moving as if to touch her, then suddenly drawing back.*)

VIVIANNE. Come on, kid, you're just as tired as I am. If you don't make it snappy, I shall put the light off and you'll have to undress in the dark. (*Thumps mattress viciously.*) It's not such a bad bed.

CHRISTINE (*sobbing*). I can't stay here—I can't.

VIVIANNE. Oh, come on.

CHRISTINE. I've never lived like this before.

VIVIANNE (*crossing to divan L.*). Most of us had something better, once.

CHRISTINE. This place frightens me. I want to get my baby out of here to-night.

VIVIANNE. Don't be silly—they'd run you in. (*Puts sponge bag and towel on cupboard top, then turns back bed-clothes.*) Come on—get into bed.

> (*CHRISTINE rises—still sobbing. VIVIANNE waits a minute then sits on her own bed.*)

VIVIANNE. Funny, when you get to a certain pitch you begin to appreciate the animal comforts of just sleeping and eating —even in a place like this. I suppose there's nothing else.

CHRISTINE (*with sudden determination*). I'll get up very early.

VIVIANNE. You bet you will.

CHRISTINE. I'll get up very early and I'll find another place. I'm bound to find somewhere if I search all day.

VIVIANNE. That's what they all say, but they never do.

CHRISTINE. I'll find somewhere to-morrow.

VIVIANNE. Maybe you'll tramp the streets for an hour or so, then you'll get fed up and decide to try the next day, and the next day, and the next. And after you've tramped a good many miles, you'll get around to thinking maybe this is not so bad. You'll find yourself wondering if you're not lucky after all, and in a little while you'll stop at home and not bother looking any more.

CHRISTINE. No—no.

VIVIANNE (*stretching sleepily*). Yes, you will. It's the same with all of us.

CHRISTINE. No, it isn't. I'm not going to live like this. It's only till to-morrow.

VIVIANNE (*laughs*). I'm going to turn the light off. (*Slips out of bed and crosses to the switch by door* L.) Hurry up and get into bed.

CHRISTINE (*fiercely*). It's only till to-morrow—do you understand?

(VIVIANNE *laughs again*—CHRISTINE *fiercely—with a sob.*)
It's only till to-morrow.

(*She turns to look at* VIVIANNE *who touches the switch and the stage is plunged into darkness.*)

QUICK CURTAIN

ACT I

SCENE 2

The same a few weeks later.

The clothes-horse had been moved away from the fire and folded against cupboard R. of it. A third divan has been placed down R. below the door leading to the kitchen leaving very little space for movement. SAL, a slovenly creature whose age is difficult to determine, is sitting on the L. side of it, peeling potatoes into a bowl. When she speaks, her words are laboured and uncertain and it is obvious that she is mentally below average. JESSIE is lounging on the divan L. VERONICA, a very pretty, well-dressed girl of eighteen, is sitting L. of table reading a magazine. At the opposite side OLGA—a black-haired, heavily made-up girl of about twenty-eight, is varnishing her toe-nails dark red.

VERONICA. Must you do that in here? The smell of that stuff always makes me feel sick.

OLGA. Where else am I supposed to do it? This is my bed-room. If you don't like it, you'd better go upstairs.

VERONICA. It happens to be our sitting-room as well.

JESSIE. Go easy on them, Sal. It's the spuds we're figurin' on eating, not the skins. Rosie's late, ain't she? I'm stoppin' in to-morrow night to get 'er 'air ready for the weddin'.

VERONICA (*loftily*). I suppose they're going to Margate for their honeymoon. It will be rather awkward having to explain the baby.

JESSIE. They'll tell the landlady they found it under a goose-berry bush—same as you found yours.

VERONICA. It was a lilac bush.

JESSIE. Ever so refined!

VERONICA. And I didn't find it, I was raped.

JESSIE. Got no sense of 'umour, that girl.

VERONICA. Daddy would have taken him to Court—only——

JESSIE. Only you wasn't sure which one it was.

VERONICA. Not at all! A man in my father's position couldn't risk the publicity.

OLGA. Is Rosie really gettin' married?

JESSIE. Sure—Saturday dinner time. We're all invited to the weddin', Registry Office of course, but we're 'avin' a bit of a binge in the George and Dragon afterwards.

OLGA. Poor bitch.

JESSIE. Eh?

OLGA. I wouldn't be in her shoes for a million pounds. Men are the biggest mistake on God's earth.

JESSIE (*stretching*). Oh no—men's lovely.

VERONICA (*darkly to* OLGA). Where would you be without them?

JESSIE. Catches on quick for a girl who's only just found out the facts of life.

(CHRISTINE *enters* L. *She has an apron over her dress and her sleeves are rolled up.*)

CHRISTINE. Is Vivianne in yet?

JESSIE. Ain't seen 'er.

CHRISTINE (*going to mirror above mantelpiece*). Christopher's being a little beast. Mrs. Allistair says he goes to sleep as good as gold when she puts him to bed, but just because it's my half day he's taking advantage.

JESSIE. Shove 'im in the cot and let 'im yell. (*To* SAL.) Ain't those spuds done yet? Well, don't expect 'em to walk into the kitchen and put themselves in a pan. Really you get soppier every day. Go on. Get movin'.

(SAL *walks slowly to the kitchen.*)

VERONICA. I'm sure that girl ought to be put away. She gives me the creeps. If Mummy had seen her, I'm sure she'd never have let me stay here.

OLGA. That would be a great loss to us all.

VERONICA (*looking out of the window* C.). It's clearing up. I'll bet my friends are playing tennis at the Club to-night. There's a little bar there—only soft drinks served, of course—but we used to have some lovely times.

JESSIE. I'll bet you did.

VERONICA. I wish I could go home.

JESSIE. And 'ave all the neighbours peepin' at you from be'ind their curtains, trying to figure where the little stranger came from.

VERONICA. They'd know it wasn't my fault. Daddy never let me go with anyone outside the Youth Club.

OLGA. What's the bettin'? They'd be blaming the curate!

VERONICA. Oh no—Mr. Bradbury never went as far as that.

OLGA. If my guess is right you was a girl guide, too.

JESSIE (*rises*). Well—it's time I went and made myself look beautiful. When Rosie comes in, tell her that the spuds are in and she's only got to 'eat the 'ash up.

(*Goes out* L.)

OLGA (*rising and going to divan* R, *where she finds her handbag—and proceeds to make-up her face*). Hash again! I'm only thankful we don't know what goes into it. Do you know that Nellie Allistair has meat five days a week, and chicken on Sunday?

CHRISTINE (*trying to tidy newspapers lying on floor by divan* L.). Does she?

OLGA. And have you ever stopped to think it's our meat ration?

CHRISTINE. What can we do about it?

OLGA. That's just it—we can't do anything. I tell you straight, I'd starve to death on what she gives us if I didn't eat up town. You know what, Chris, you ought to get a boy friend—just to make life easier till your Ron comes home. I could introduce you to a lot of fellows.

CHRISTINE. No, thanks.

OLGA. It's no use being soft in this world. Men are only good

for what you can get out of them. Use 'em while you can.
Have a damn good time yourself—and keep your wits about
you. Then later, when you're getting on, you can tell the lot
of them to go to hell. I've got my little nest-egg put away
and, what's more, Nellie isn't going to get her hands on it.

CHRISTINE. What about your child?

OLGA. The kid's all right, as long as I've got money. I'll bring
her up to be a little lady. A kid's a good investment—better
than a man.

(*Breaks off as* VIVIANNE *enters* L. *in outdoor clothes—
smart but unsuitable for rain. She looks very pale and, though
quite calm, less self-assured than in the last scene.*)

Hullo, sunshine!

VIVIANNE. Hullo.

(*Crosses to the table, throwing down her handbag and
gloves. Crosses to her bed and sits down.*)

OLGA. How did it go to-day?

(*As* VIVIANNE *does not answer.*)

You know, I don't agree with murder, but when it comes to
a showdown my sympathies are always with the fellow in
the dock. Maybe it's because I've been inside myself. .

VERONICA (*coming down above table*). In prison! You don't
mean it?

OLGA. Sure I have—but they never kept me very long.

VERONICA (*returning to window* C.). I'm going to write to
Daddy again. He couldn't make me stay here if he knew.
What have I done to deserve it?

OLGA. Don't you know yet?

(ROSIE *enters breathlessly* L. *She has been running and
looks flushed and angry.*)

ROSIE. Where is she—where's Nellie Allistair?

OLGA (*sitting in chair* R. *of table*). Search me.

ROSIE. Bert says I've got to have her up in Court—I've got to
tell 'em everything. Undernourished, they said—suffering
from malnu—malnu something or other.

VERONICA. Malnutrition.

ROSIE. Yes—that was it. (*She is* L.C.)

CHRISTINE (*going to her*). Who said that?

ROSIE. The people at the clinic: they made me take 'im to the 'ospital. Bert says I've got to go back there to-morrow, and tell 'em as 'ow I pay Nellie thirty bob a week to look after 'im. (*Breaks off almost in tears.*) And I was goin' to take 'im to Margate on Sat'day.

CHRISTINE. I don't suppose they'll keep him long. How long is it since the last time you took him to the clinic?

ROSIE. I dunno. Jessie is supposed to take 'im once a week, but I guess she missed a few times. I wouldn't have took him to-day, only Laura was goin' with Barbie. They didn't say nothing about 'er 'avin' mal—mal—what is it?

OLGA. I don't suppose they would. Laura's smart enough to drop Jessie an extra ten bob on pay day to make sure Barbie gets what's good for her.

CHRISTINE. Don't worry, Rosie, I'm sure there can't be much the matter with him. He'll get the best attention at the hospital.

ROSIE. We was goin' to take 'im on the beach and give 'im a ride on a donkey. (*After a pause.*) 'e didn't seem bad— only a bit dopey.

(SAL *enters* R.—*stares.*)

SAL (*curiously at* ROSIE). What's she cryin' for?

CHRISTINE (*crossing to* SAL). Her baby's sick. They kept him at the hospital because they say he doesn't get enough to eat. You give the children their dinners, don't you Sal? Maybe you can tell us exactly what they have.

SAL (*blankly*). What?

CHRISTINE (*patiently*). You give Alfie his dinner, don't you?

SAL (*dully*). If they don't eat their dinner they die. Babies die if they don't eat.

(HELEN *enters* L., *sees* ROSIE'S *tears and pauses.*)

HELEN. What's the trouble now?

ROSIE. I'll tell you what the trouble is: you've been starvin'
my Alfie to death.

HELEN. I beg your pardon?

CHRISTINE. The people at the clinic sent him to the hospital;
they wouldn't let her take him home.

HELEN (sharply). Why not?

ROSIE. Because 'e's undernourished and 'as come out in spots;
only that isn't malnutrition—that's bed bugs.

HELEN (coming down to L. of ROSIE). I've never heard such
wicked lies—I suppose you had the impertinence to tell
them that.

ROSIE. Not yet, but I'm goin' to. My Bert says I've got to
have you up in Court.

HELEN. On what charge, may I ask?

ROSIE. On a charge of neglecting my Alfie.

HELEN. Then Bert is a very stupid, ignorant young man.

ROSIE. 'e isn't. I'll tell 'em everything. I'll tell 'em 'ow you
take our money and our rations, and 'ardly give us anything
to eat. I'll tell 'em 'ow the nursery stinks, and 'ow the sheets
is never changed unless you know the Welfare's comin'.

HELEN. Hold your tongue.

ROSIE (sobbing). It isn't my fault Alfie's backward. I done
everything I could for 'im. I pay you all my wages but ten
bob.

(She sinks into chair L. of table.)

HELEN (collects baby clothes from clothes-horse above fireplace). For
heaven's sake stop snivelling. If conditions in this house
aren't all they might be, it's because you girls prefer to live
like animals. You don't try to keep the place clean or take
any pride in your surroundings. As for Alfie, it's nonsense
that he's suffering from undernourishment. He may be weak
and sickly, but that's the result of generations of squalor and
ignorance and unwholesome stock. If you were worried
about him, why didn't you take him to the clinic every

W.T.—C

week, as Laura does with Barbara? You can save yourself the trouble of going to the authorities, I'll speak to them myself to-morrow morning. You might also mention to that impetuous young man of yours that I'd planned a little wedding breakfast for you on Saturday. Providing you apologise for all those stupid libellous remarks you made just now, it's still at your disposal. In the meantime, go and wash your face. Sally, I want you to light a fire in my sitting-room, and tell Jessie I'd like.to speak to her.

(*She moves towards hall door.* SAL *crosses to fireplace for bucket etc. and goes out* L.)

CHRISTINE (*above table* C.). Mrs. Allistair.

HELEN. Yes, Christine.

CHRISTINE. If what they say at the clinic is true, it's rather a serious matter.

HELEN. Do you suggest that your child's undernourished.

CHRISTINE. Some of the babies upstairs look as if they might be ailing.

HELEN. Some of the mothers were not in a condition to produce model babies. The Welfare people know the sort of home they come from. You've only to look out in the garden to see that healthy trees produce healthy fruit. Is there anything else you want to say to me?

CHRISTINE (*with a sigh*). No.

(*Exit* HELEN L.)

OLGA. She's too bloody clever.

VERONICA (*sitting in chair above table*). She may be right though; look at the children in the slums.

OLGA. Oh, shut up! You haven't turned out so wonderful yourself in spite of your fancy upbringing.

VERONICA. What do you mean?

OLGA. I mean you're just the same as all the rest of us.

VERONICA. You're quite wrong there. I told you—I was raped.

ROSIE. Yes, we know 'ow that 'appened. You didn't fall—
you was pushed.

OLGA. Right under a lilac bush.

> (VERONICA *rises angrily as* OLGA *and* CHRISTINE *laugh
> and* VIVIANNE *smiles slightly.*)

VERONICA. Oh, I hate the lot of you.

> (*Cries, makes as if to rush out* R., *but* CHRISTINE *catches
> her arm. Bursting into tears.*) I'm so miserable.

ROSIE (*a little abashed, takes her arm*). I didn't mean to upset
you—honest. There's nothing wrong in bein' raped. Look
—come and 'elp me to get the supper. We'll 'ave a nice quiet
cuppa while we do it.

> (*Leads* VERONICA *to* R.—*exeunt together.*)

OLGA (*rising lazily*). Well—seeing as the rain's stopped, I think
I'll take a little stroll. (*She moves below table towards door* L.,
swinging her hips slightly.) You might leave the scullery
window open—just a crack, in case I get back late.

> (*Winks at* CHRISTINE *meaningly and gets her coat from
> behind the door.*)

So long, kids. (*Exit* L.)

CHRISTINE (*unrolling the sleeves of her dress and crossing to*
VIVIANNE). This place gets more like bedlam every day. I
really look forward to the weeks I'm transferred to the
Brighton shop—even though it does mean leaving Christopher. I'd never have thought a drab little room in a dreary
commercial hotel could seem so much like heaven.

> (*Breaks off to look at* VIVIANNE, *who is sitting very still,
> her face averted.*)

Is anything the matter?

> (*As* VIVIANNE *laughs shortly.*)

I'm sorry, pet—it must seem a ridiculous question at a time
like this. (*After a pause—curiously.*) Are you crying?

VIVIANNE (*sharply*). No.

CHRISTINE (*to break an awkward silence*). I had a letter from Ron to-day. I'm afraid he won't be home quite as soon as he expected.

VIVIANNE (*with an effort*). Oh.

CHRISTINE (*sitting on divan* L.). If he came at once it would mean losing his promotion. I think it would be best for him to wait a little while—don't you?

VIVIANNE. I don't know.

CHRISTINE. Of course, I want him to come home, but if he lost his job——

(VIVANNE *turns away covering her eyes with her hand.*)

Something's happened—tell me.

VIVIANNE. The trial ended to-day.

CHRISTINE. Oh, my dear, how selfish—I hadn't realised.

VIVIANNE (*in a whisper*). Guilty.

CHRISTINE. I'm so very sorry.

VIVIANNE. Are you? Everyone else seems delighted. Oh, God! Now that it's over I shan't ever see him again.

CHRISTINE. Darling.

VIVIANNE (*staring in front of her*). He looked straight at me when they passed the verdict. He'd never looked at me before—not all that time. Then, just before they took him out, he smiled the way he used to.

CHRISTINE. Can I get you anything? You look so white.

VIVIANNE. Some water, could you?

CHRISTINE. You'd better take that coat off—it's soaked through.

(VIVIANNE *allows* CHRISTINE *to help her off with it. Exit* CHRISTINE *to the kitchen.* VIVIANNE *puts the coat over the back of the chair and sinks down on the bed again—the jewelled bracelet slips off her wrist on to the floor. She moves to retrieve it, then sways back dizzily, covering her face with her hands. The bracelet is left on the floor by the divan.* CHRISTINE *enters with a glass of water and gives it to* VIVIANNE *who drinks a little and gives the glass back to* CHRISTINE *who puts it on the table.*)

Better?

VIVIANNE. Thanks—I was thirsty. I fainted in the Court this afternoon.

(*As* CHRISTINE *exclaims in sympathy.*)

The place was full of pressmen—some of them even followed me into a café afterwards—wanted me to write the story of my life with Johnny, for a Sunday paper.

CHRISTINE. You wouldn't?

VIVIANNE. Of course not. That would be a nice beginning for my child.

CHRISTINE. Johnny can appeal—I think they always do.

VIVIANNE. Not Johnny, he knows when he's beaten.

CHRISTINE. I expect they'll let you see him. You could tell him about the child.

VIVIANNE. Do you know what he'd do? He'd laugh like hell.

CHRISTINE. Laugh?

VIVIANNE. Yes—he'd laugh at me for being such a bloody fool, for getting caught—for messing up my life. I can hear him say it—" You know where to go—you know what to do ".

CHRISTINE (*sharply, crossing to sit on divan* L.). Vivianne, stop it —don't. You'd have wanted his baby, wouldn't you, if you could have lived with him an honest, decent life?

VIVIANNE (*wearily*). Perhaps—I don't know.

CHRISTINE. It's not as if he were a criminal when you fell in love with him.

VIVIANNE. No—he was an out of work actor. Since then, he's been an out of work salesman, an out of work clerk, an out of work waiter.

CHRISTINE. You deserved something better.

VIVIANNE. For heaven's sake, don't be sympathetic—there's nothing anyone can do. (*She pauses, and then says quietly.*) I wanted Johnny, that's all.

CHRISTINE (*rising—takes* VIVIANNE'S *dressing-gown from under the pillow*). You can go and have a nice hot bath while I get supper.

VIVIANNE. I don't want a nice hot bath and I couldn't possibly eat any supper. (*Crosses* L., *taking dressing-gown*.)

(ROSIE *enters* R.)

CHRISTINE. You won't mind going upstairs right after supper this once, will you, Rosie? Vivianne isn't feeling very well.

ROSIE (*dismally*). No—I don't mind—I was goin' to get the machine out and finish them rompers I was making for Alfie at Margate, but 'e won't be needin' 'em now. (*She sits on table* C.)

CHRISTINE (*crossing behind table to chair* R. *of it*). Cheer up, ducky, —I'm sure he'll soon be well.

ROSIE. Nellie thinks I'm goin' to let 'er get away with it just because I'm leavin', but I won't.

CHRISTINE. I should be careful if I were you: she's very clever.

VIVIANNE. You bet she is. Somehow she'll manage to shift the blame on you. (*Coming back towards* ROSIE—*with meaning*.)

CHRISTINE. Have you spoken to Jess about it? She's with the kids all day, and she's hand in glove with Nellie Allistair.

ROSIE (*surprised*). Jess is my pal.

VIVIANNE. I wouldn't be too sure of that. Can't say I've noticed any signs of her Marlene dying of starvation. Who cooks the food and doles it out? It's not surprising that she avoided taking Alfie to the clinic for the past few weeks.

(*The hall door opens slightly, and we see* JESSIE *standing there, eavesdropping*.)

ROSIE. But she thinks the world of Alfie.

VIVIANNE. And think still more of him if you were to tip her ten bob a week.

ROSIE. She knows I can't do that—I haven't got it.

VIVIANNE. Even Christine takes the precaution of slipping her a little present now and then. Sorry, Chris—but you can't deny it, can you?

CHRISTINE (*unhappily*). I don't agree with it, but it seems the only way.

ROSIE. Gawd—if I thought she didn't treat my Alfie right I'd knock her teeth in, pal or no pal.

(JESSIE *enters; shutting door behind her. She is wearing a gaudy dressing-gown and bedroom slippers.*)

JESSIE. Talk of the devil, eh? I 'eard what you was saying. You thought I was in the bedroom, didn't you? But I wasn't, see, I was listening outside. (*Crosses and strikes* VIVIANNE *across the face with sudden fury.*) Well, that's to teach you that I don't like mischief makers.

(VIVIANNE *does not move but returns her glare steadily.*)

VIVIANNE. It was the truth. You wouldn't have stopped here all these years if Nellie hadn't made you a party to her little schemes. You're just as crooked as she is, only we know where we are with her and you pretend to be on our side.

JESSIE (*threateningly*). Ain't you 'ad enough?

CHRISTINE (*as she comes to* VIVIANNE). Leave her alone—she isn't well. Haven't you any sense of decency?

JESSIE. You keep out of this.

VIVIANNE. It's all right, Chris, I'm not afraid of her.

CHRISTINE. Come upstairs.

VIVIANNE. It wouldn't suit you, would it, if Rosie really went to the authorities?

JESSIE. Listen! I ain't warning you again: you keep your bloody trap shut.

CHRISTINE. Come on.

(*Puts her arm round* VIVIANNE *as she falters a little, supporting herself against the door.* VIVIANNE *hesitates, still glaring at* JESSIE, *then allows herself to be led off by* CHRISTINE. *Exeunt* L.)

JESSIE (*deeply hurt*). Knock my teeth in would you, Rosie? Me, who's always been your pal. Why! I looked after Alfie like one of me own.

ROSIE (*rising*). Did Nellie tell you what they said about 'im at the clinic?

JESSIE (*collecting cigarette from vase on mantelpiece*). I'll say she did: I got to stop at 'ome and clean this place out, just when I was looking forward to a nice evenin' at the Palais. You are soppy, honestly. Why couldn't you 'ave waited until after you got back from Margate? There ain't nothing wrong with Alfie. Those nosy parkers got to tell you somethin', seeing as they get paid to interfere.

ROSIE. Oh no—they put 'im on the scales and weighed 'im. He's a scraggy as a sparrow when you got 'is clothes off.

JESSIE. Alfie's wiry like my Georgie was when 'e was little. They kicked up something awful cos 'is legs was crooked, but you should see 'im climb a tree, just like a bleeding monkey, and as tough as nails. Come and 'elp me fill the boiler up, we'll need plenty of 'ot water if we're goin' to scrub the house out. (*She moves to* ROSIE'S *left*).

ROSIE. What we got to do that for?

JESSIE. Why, in case the Welfare comes, silly. You don't think Nellie's goin' to let them see the place like a pigsty?

ROSIE (*stolidly*). I ain't goin' to do no scrubbin'. Why should I 'elp cover up fer 'er? Let the Welfare see it like it always is.

JESSIE. You ain't 'arf selfish, Rosie Gordon. Just because you got a place to live, you'll see us all turned out in the streets.

(*The last few words are said slowly and mechanically as she catches sight of the bracelet which* VIVIANNE *has dropped. She kicks it surreptitiously under the bed.*)

ROSIE (*who has seen this*). Well, what are you waitin' fer?

JESSIE. Eh?

ROSIE. Thought you was goin' to put the boiler on.

(JESSIE *nods and goes reluctantly to kitchen.* ROSIE *kneels by bed and gropes under it for the bracelet which she finds, and holds up to the light.* JESSIE, *returning immediately, sees this, and starts angrily.*)

JESSIE. What you go there?

ROSIE (*startled, thrusts bracelet into her pocket*). Nothin'.

JESSIE. Yes, you 'ave; I saw you shoving somethin' in your pocket.

ROSIE. Nothin' to do with you.

JESSIE. Come off it, Rosie—I'm your pal.

ROSIE. I ain't so sure of that.

(*As* JESSIE *catches hold of her arm to detain her.*)

Get out of the way, I'm goin' to finish the supper. (*Exit to kitchen.*)

(JESSIE *watches her then looks quickly at the spot where she has seen the bracelet—grins suddenly and sits on divan* R. CHRISTINE *enters* L., *her arms full of packages.* HELEN *follows briskly, carrying some laundry, baby-linen, etc.*)

HELEN (*brightly*). Out of the way—out of the way—I've got work to do. Did you fill the boiler, Jess? Put plenty of carbolic in the water, it'll make the place smell fresh. You'll have to move the cots on to the landing while you scrub the nursery. (*She is above table* C.)

(*To* CHRISTINE *who puts her parcels of food on to the left of the table.*)

Has Vivianne come home yet?

CHRISTINE (*briefly*). She's in the bathroom.

HELEN. There was a picture of her in this evening's paper. I wonder if she's seen it.

CHRISTINE. Don't show it to her, please. Let her try to forget for a little while.

HELEN. She really photographs awfully well. Hello! Someone's going to have a feast.

CHRISTINE. I was going to give Vivianne her supper in bed— she doesn't eat enough.

HELEN. You'll be accusing me of starving her next.

CHRISTINE. Some of the stuff you give us isn't fit for pigs.

HELEN (*calmly*). We do the best we can under present-day restrictions. If it's good enough for the rest of us, it's good enough for her.

CHRISTINE. Mrs. Allistair, Vivianne isn't well. She fainted in the Court to-day.

HELEN. Fainted? Did she? Well, I've already told her she ought to look after herself—I can't do with invalids here.

CHRISTINE. I was wondering: could you put her in your little guest room? It's hardly ever used, and it does seem a pity that she has to be disturbed so early in the morning.

HELEN. Put her in the guest room! I never heard such nonsense. Next thing you'll be asking me to take her breakfast up to bed.

CHRISTINE. That wouldn't be such a fantastic request, considering the amount we have to pay here.

JESSIE. I'd put 'er out on the streets, if I 'ad my way.

CHRISTINE (*sharply*). Well you haven't got your way, and if you dare so much as lay a finger on her again I'll—I'll knock your teeth in.

(HELEN *and* JESSIE *stare at her surprised;* JESSIE *bursts out laughing.*)

HELEN (*seeing a tin amongst* CHRISTINE's *packages*). My goodness—are those strawberries?

CHRISTINE. They are.

HELEN. I suppose you couldn't spare me some? I've invited a friend round for supper to-night. It would be such a treat for her.

CHRISTINE (*hands them to her grimly*). All right.

HELEN. That is sweet of you.

CHRISTINE. I thought I'd share the butter among the children— and they need it more than I do.

HELEN. What a charming thought. You better let me take it, my dear, and I'll see it is evenly distributed. If you leave it down here, the girls will wolf the lot. (*Takes package from* CHRISTINE *who hands it over distrustfully.*)

JESSIE. Anything for me?

CHRISTINE. You can take those sweets if you like—but make sure the others get some. (*She tosses* JESSIE *a small package.*)

(VIVIANNE *enters looking pale and worried. She crosses to her bed* L. *and looks around the floor.*)

What's the matter?

VIVIANNE. Has anyone seen my bracelet?

CHRISTINE. Oh, Viv, you haven't lost it?

VIVIANNE. No, it fell off when I was sitting on the bed. Perhaps it's underneath.

(CHRISTINE *looks underneath bed, on* L. *side of it.*)

No? That's funny, I noticed where I dropped it.

HELEN. If you noticed, why didn't you pick it up?

VIVIANNE. I—didn't bother and later I forgot. (*To* CHRISTINE.) Have you looked properly?

CHRISTINE. Yes, darling—I'm quite sure.

JESSIE (*sitting up*). Is it that fancy one with the rubies?

VIVIANNE. Yes.

HELEN. Really, dear, you ought to be careful: a valuable thing like that. It isn't that I don't trust the girls, but you are rather putting temptation in their way.

CHRISTINE. You're certain you dropped it in here?

VIVIANNE. Absolutely certain; I was sitting on the bed.

HELEN. You haven't seen it, have you, Jess?

JESSIE (*thoughtfully*). No.

HELEN. Who else has been in since?

JESSIE (*with mock-reluctance*). No one—that is—only Rosie. ·

CHRISTINE (*to* JESSIE). You're sure you haven't seen it?

JESSIE. Are you callin' me a liar?

CHRISTINE. No—but it can't have walked away.

JESSIE. Wait a minute—now I come to think—Rosie did pick up something off the floor—I'd just come in from the kitchen, and when I asked 'er what it was she shoved it in 'er pocket.

(VIVIANNE *sits wearily on the bed.*)

HELEN. You'd better call her.

(JESSIE *calls off for* ROSIE—ROSIE *enters* R. *almost at once and stands glaring suspiciously at* HELEN.)

I'd like to speak to you a minute, Rosie.

ROSIE (*crossing to* HELEN *above table*). If it's about the Welfare, I've 'ad my say. I'm going to do what Bertie told me. (*With a meaning glance at* JESSIE.) I don't care who gets dragged in.

HELEN. No—it's not about that. (*Crosses to her swiftly, taking her arm.*) I want to see what's in your pockets.

(ROSIE *struggles as* HELEN *investigates the pockets of her overall.*)

ROSIE. Hey, what do you think you're doin'?

HELEN. There.

(*Holds up bracelet for the others to see.* VIVIANNE *looks indifferent—she seems to have lost interest.* JESSIE *gasps.*)

JESSIE. Well I never! Whoever would 'ave thought it?

HELEN. That's your bracelet, isn't it, Vivianne?

ROSIE. Course it's 'ers. So what? I was only keepin' it for 'er. (*She moves down to* VIVIANNE.) I found it on the floor: I was goin' to give it to you when you come down.

JESSIE. Then why did you 'ave to 'ide it?

ROSIE. 'cos I wanted 'er to get it back. (*To* VIVIANNE.) You believe me, don't you?

VIVIANNE (*with a shrug*). It's not important.

HELEN. I'm afraid that's where you're wrong. There have been several thefts brought to my attention lately—nothing as serious as this. You know that people can be sent to prison for stealing, don't you, Rosie?

ROSIE. I wasn't stealin'.

HELEN. You were caught behaving in a very suspicious manner. As Jess said, there was no earthly reason for concealing the bracelet if you intended to return it. However, as you'll soon be leaving us I'll let you off this time providing, of course, Vivianne does not wish to bring a charge against you.

VIVIANNE. I've no intention of charging anyone with anything.

JESSIE. I should think you bloody well 'aven't—seein' as it was probably stolen in the first place.

VIVIANNE. Johnny gave it to me.

JESSIE. That's what I mean.

HELEN. Very well—we'll let the matter drop. It would be a pity to think of Rosie going to gaol instead of on her honeymoon. (*To* ROSIE, *smiling.*) We won't let anything spoil that little wedding breakfast I was planning will we, Rosie?

ROSIE (*sullenly*). No.

HELEN. I like my girls to part with me on friendly terms—to feel their stay here has been a pleasant one—but I'm sure you'll make that clear to everyone.

ROSIE. You mean the Welfare?

HELEN. I mean anyone who happens to ask. (*She takes bracelet out of her pocket and looks at it.*)

ROSIE (*after a pause*). Yes—I got you.

HELEN. I rather thought you would. (*Hall clock strikes.*) That's splendid! Oh dear, I'm afraid supper's going to be awfully late. We'd better get it over as quickly as possible: we've got a lot to do to-night, but it won't take long if everyone lends a hand.

JESSIE. It would 'ave to be to-night—I 'ad a date with ever such a smashing feller.

HELEN (*to* ROSIE). All right, Rosie, you carry on.

(*Exit* ROSIE *to kitchen*—CHRISTINE *gathers up her parcels.*)

JESSIE (*rising*). I could kill Rosie, takin' 'er kid to the Clinic and causing all this fuss.

CHRISTINE. Don't be too long, Viv—I'm having my supper in here with you. (*She goes into kitchen.*)

HELEN. Go and put some clothes on, Jess—you can't work like that.

JESSIE. Can't I?

HELEN (*with a glance at* VIVIANNE). It doesn't look as though we're going to get much assistance. Where's Olga?

JESSIE. Out on the bash again—I shouldn't wonder.

HELEN (*lightly*). Really? Oh well, it can't be helped.

(*Exit* JESSIE R.)

(*To* VIVIANNE.) I saw the result of the case in to-night's paper; you mustn't take it too hard—you know you have a friend in me.

(*She takes baby-linen from table and puts it on clothes-horse before the fire.*)

VIVIANNE (*wearily, turning away*). Yes—yes—that's very nice—but let's not talk about it at the moment.

HELEN. I have some news for you. I was able to contact a friend of mine to-day—a midwife—she has a little cottage not far out of town. When I explained your circumstances to her, and how you have a horror of going into hospital because of the attention you might attract, she agreed to let you have your baby there. It's perfectly in order; I knew her in my nursing days. She's fully qualified, and very kind.

VIVIANNE. When shall I have to go to her?

HELEN. Oh, not for months yet—about a couple of weeks before the baby is due.

VIVIANNE. Will it cost me very much?

HELEN. You must settle that with her. I had to pay a small sum in advance—just to book your room, you know. You can give that to me, but the rest must be decided between you two. (HELEN *sits on* L. *side of divan. After a pause as* VIVIANNE *is silent.*)

I thought that would be a load off your mind.

VIVIANNE. Yes—I'm very grateful.

HELEN. You'll have to take better care of yourself in the meantime, though, it's only fair to my friend. Have you enough money to live on until the baby comes?

VIVIANNE. I can get a job. If the worst comes to the worst I could wash dishes in a restaurant. I don't suppose anyone would be looking for me there. (*She crosses to* R. *of table for matches.*)

HELEN (*shaking her head slowly*). You'd never stand up to it, my dear, long hours—being on your feet all day—you'd soon crock up. No, the best thing you can do is stop and help me here—I could do with some assistance in the nursery. Of course, I'm assuming that you have a little money behind you. There's no truth in the report that you've been offered quite a large amount to write your story for the newspapers?

VIVIANNE (*sharply*). No, there isn't.

HELEN. I often hear of childless couples who long for a baby.

VIVIANNE (*turning to her*). Is that part of your business?

HELEN (*startled*). What?

VIVIANNE. Baby farming.

HELEN. I don't know what you're talking about.

VIVIANNE. Oh yes you do, Mrs. Allistair, you know perfectly well and there's nothing doing. You'll get your rent money each week; where it comes from is none of your business. I'm not selling my story to the papers and I'm not bartering my child.

HELEN (*rising and controlling her temper with an effort*). Jess is quite right—you're ungrateful and insolent. I've got a long list of girls who'd be only too glad to have your bed. More —I have gone to all this trouble to get you fixed up with my friend—I've offered you a job here—offered to look after you——

(*Breaks off suddenly, aware of the weariness and defeat in* VIVIANNE'S *attitude. She stands with her back to* HELEN, *covering her face with her hands by chair* R. *of table.*)

VIVIANNE (*in a whisper*). I'm so tired—I've never been so tired before.

HELEN (*in an altered tone*). Of course I wouldn't turn you out. In all these years I've never turned a girl away. You ought to go to bed and get some rest.

VIVIANNE. How am I to do that if they're going to start a cleaning campaign.

HELEN. We won't touch this room till the morning. Run

along now and have a nice warm bath: Chris will bring
you your supper. (*Crosses to her, and pushes her gently towards
door* L.)

VIVIANNE (*turns in doorway, suddenly remembering*). Oh, may I
have my bracelet, please?

HELEN. I'd—forgotten. (*Takes the bracelet from her pocket.*) It's
pretty, isn't it? Worth quite a lot of money—I think perhaps I ought to keep it, don't you?

(*There is a long pause—*VIVIANNE *looks at her, but does
not move.*)

VIVIANNE. I understand.

HELEN. I hope you do, my dear. After all, I'm not a wealthy
woman.

VIVIANNE. I understand perfectly.

(*Stares at the bracelet for a moment, then turns abruptly and
goes out* L. HELEN *stands examining her trinket with satisfaction. Almost at once* JESSIE *enters* R. *Suddenly she laughs
aloud.*)

JESSIE (*slapping her on the shoulder. Holds out her hand grinning*).
Come on—hand over.

HELEN (*uncertainly*). No.

JESSIE. Fifty-fifty! I'll flog it first thing in the morning.

(HELEN *hands it to her reluctantly.* JESSIE *laughs again
loudly and gives her another slap on the back.*)
You old cow!

The CURTAIN *falls on* JESSIE'S *raucous laughter.*

ACT II

SCENE I

The same, about a month later.

When the curtain rises, JESSIE, *with her hair in curlers, is sitting at the table which is set for breakfast. There is a loaf on the table, a sticky jam jar, a bottle of milk beside a stack of dirty crockery.* OLGA *is sitting sleepily on her unmade bed down* R., *combing her hair.*

She is smoking a cigarette which she lays on a saucer from time to time while coping with the worst tangles. LAURA, *fresh and neatly dressed, is packing a small fibre trunk on the divan down* L.

They all maintain a rather touchy silence which is broken by SAL'S *noisy entrance* L. *with a tea-tray.*

JESSIE. That's it, dear. If you got to smash a cup, smash that one. It's the last one of the set 'er granny gave 'er for a weddin' present.

SAL. Got to take 'er another pot of tea.

JESSIE. Why's that?

SAL (*putting tea-tray on table*). Says water wasn't on the boil— tea leaves floatin' on the top.

JESSIE. Damned good pot of tea you'd make without 'em. 'ear that? Who made Nellie's tea this mornin'?

LAURA. It was Olga—wasn't it?

JESSIE. Olga, Nellie don't like 'er tea with leaves in it. Life isn't worth living if she starts the day without 'er early mornin' cuppa. (*Moves to radio on dresser.*)

OLGA (*blankly*). What 'ave I done wrong this time?

JESSIE. Put leaves in Nellie's tea and she don't like 'em.

(*Switches wireless on—there is a blare of music. The response is definitely hostile.*)

OLGA. Then she can do without. I'm not her chambermaid.

LAURA. For heaven's sake turn that thing off—I can't hear myself think. Do you think you could dress Barbara for me, Sal? The taxi's coming at eight and I've still quite a lot of packing to do.

OLGA (*switching radio off*). Bet you'll be sorry to see the last of us!

JESSIE. You'll let us know 'ow you get on in your posh flat, won't you?

LAURA. Yes, of course. You'll have to come and visit me. (*Hurriedly.*) Would you mind, Sal? You'll have to put her best coat on. It's the only one I haven't packed.

SAL (*crossing to* L.). Must go and dress Barbie. Barbie's going away. (*Exit* L.)

(OLGA *stands over the table, combing her hair.*)

JESSIE. We don't really want your hair in the marmalade.

OLGA. I got to comb it somewhere, haven't I? This is my bedroom.

JESSIE. Then you can bloody well wait until I've finished eating.

OLGA. You've got all day ahead of you—I have to be down town by nine o'clock. Damned silly time to open a shop. Who in their right minds wants to buy ladies' underwear at nine o'clock? (*Stares at* JESSIE *with distaste.*) How can you eat all that at this hour?

JESSIE. Always like to start the day with a bit of something fried. It puts new 'eart into you.

(*Breaks off as* CHRISTINE *enters* L. *in a dressing-gown, with a bath towel over her arm.*)

Good morning, duchess.

OLGA (*sinking down on bed down* R.) Gawd—I'd like to go to sleep again.

JESSIE. You know; what I likes about you girls: you're all so cheerful in the morning. My Ernie's daddy used to say " Jess," 'e'd say, " you greets the dawn just like a little

lark: to look at you, anyone would think you 'adn't 'ad a
lark the night before ". (*Laughs.*) Now Marlene's dad was
quite the opposite: 'e'd clout you if you spoke to 'im before
the pubs was open.

CHRISTINE (*looking round from divan up* R.). Where's Viv?

JESSIE. Wouldn't know, dear.

OLGA. She must have gone out after you went up to the bathroom.

CHRISTINE (*startled*). Where did she go?

OLGA. I didn't ask her. Matter of fact I went to sleep again.
You were up early this morning, weren't you?

CHRISTINE. I didn't sleep too well, and there wasn't much
point in lying in bed since I was awake. What time did
Viv go out?

OLGA. I really couldn't say. The last I saw of her was just
after you went upstairs. You must have woken us both up.
(*She is making up her eyes.*)

CHRISTINE. Sorry, I tried to make as little noise as possible.
Was she all right?

OLGA. She asked me what the time was and I told her to get
up and look. Then the next thing I knew, these noisy devils
were crashing about getting breakfast—you must have been
a long time in the bathroom!

CHRISTINE (*worriedly*). I do think you might have kept an eye
on Viv this morning.

OLGA. Why should I? It's not my affair if she wants to go out
at the crack of dawn.

CHRISTINE (*angrily*). Don't you know what day it is?

OLGA. Sure—it's Thursday.

CHRISTINE. It's to-day they're hanging Johnny Stanton.
(*There is a startled silence.*)

OLGA (*genuinely upset*). I'd quite forgotten, Chris—honestly;
I'd have kept an eye on her if I'd known but—she never
tells you anything and you were both asleep when I came to
bed last night.

(VERONICA *enters* L., *fresh and pretty in a light summer dress. She comes straight to the table, pours herself out some tea and takes it to the fireplace, puts it on the mantelpiece while she stands in front of the mirror, patting her hair.*)

JESSIE. There's another one who thinks this is a beauty parlour.

VERONICA. Don't anybody speak to me, I'm late. The boss is picking me up at the corner in his car.

JESSIE. Nice work if you can get it. (*To* CHRISTINE.) Don't you want a cuppa, ducks?

CHRISTINE. I'm worried about Viv—I can't go to work until I know where she is.

LAURA. Well, there's really nothing you can do.

(VIVIANNE *enters* R. *She has an overcoat over her dressing gown and bedroom slippers on her feet. Her hair is dishevelled and she is very pale but apparently quite calm. She stands in the doorway for a moment aware of their self-conscious silence.*)

VIVIANNE (*after a pause*). Is anything the matter?

LAURA. Why no! It's just—we wondered where you were.

VIVIANNE. I was in the garden. May I have a cup of tea? (*She comes to table* C.)

JESSIE. Sure—it could do with some more water.

(*As* VIVIANNE *moves to take the teapot.*)

Don't worry, I'll get it.

(*Exit* JESSIE *to kitchen.* VIVIANNE *sits* L. *of the table.*)

VIVIANNE (*looking at* LAURA). You're leaving this morning, aren't you, Laura? You must be very pleased.

LAURA. Yes—I am—having a place of my own. I've fixed up for Barbara at a very nice little day nursery. A year ago I had so little—now I've got everything I want. (*She has packed and corded up her trunk by now.*)

VERONICA. Oh, darn my hair!

OLGA. I should darn my stockings if I were you. You've got a bloody great hole in the back.

VERONICA. Oh dear, I haven't, have I? Oh lord!

CHRISTINE (*crossing behind* VIVIANNE's *chair—quickly*). Did you sleep at all?

(VIVIANNE *shakes her head, smiling slightly. She seems rather dazed.* JESSIE *re-enters with the teapot, fills a cup and passes it to* VIVIANNE.)

JESSIE. Would you like a piece of toast?   (*Sits down again opposite* VIVIANNE.)

VIVIANNE. No, thanks. (*Drinks some tea.*) It's nice and hot. (*Shivers slightly, drawing her coat round her.*)

VERONICA. Has anyone a bit of darning silk?

(*No one answers, and she goes frantically through drawer of cupboard above fireplace, finds some, and proceeds to cobble her stocking.*)

OLGA. I think I hear the postman.

VERONICA. Go and see if there's anything for me—I'm dreadfully late.

LAURA. I'll go—I think I've packed everything now. (*She goes out* L.)

VIVIANNE (*to* OLGA). I wonder—could you lend me a cigarette?

OLGA. Sure.

(*Passes her a cigarette and lights it for her. In spite of her apparent calm,* VIVIANNE's *hands are trembling uncertainly. She fumbles so that* OLGA *has to strike a second match.*)

VIVIANNE. Sorry.

JESSIE. Shall I fill it up?

VIVIANNE (*not completely with them*). Please—I'm feeling rather cold. It's so long since I was out in the very early morning. We had a caravan one summer and we used to hear the birds start singing and see the sun come up. It reminded me——

OLGA (*with strained cheerfulness, breaking a short silence*). It's going to be a nice day—isn't it? (*She returns to her bed.*)

CHRISTINE. Hot, I should think.

JESSIE. It'll be a real scorcher by lunch-time. Thought maybe I'd take the kids down to the paddling pool.

(*Glances at* VIVIANNE, *who is leaning with her elbow on the
table, covering her eyes with the back of her hand. There is
another uneasy silence—broken by* LAURA *who enters with the
post.*)

LAURA. Two for you, Veronica, one for Chris, and a postcard
for Jess. (*She hands letters to them.*)

(VERONICA *is below divan* L.)

VIVIANNE (*quickly*). Nothing for me?

LAURA. No, I'm afraid not.

JESSIE (*glancing at her card*). It's from Rosie—wants me to go
over for tea on Sunday. Can't say as I feel like another dose
of Bertie's great aunt. Cor—what do you think? She's goin'
to 'ave another kid.

OLGA. Bertie's great aunt?

JESSIE. Blimey—ain't love grand? She sends 'er love to all of
you.

VIVIANNE. Read your letter, Chris.

(CHRISTINE *hesitates, then opens the envelope. She is
behind table* C.)

VERONICA (*gulping her tea and reading*). Oooh! it's from Alan
Clarke: he's gone and joined the Air Force—I'll kill him.
Oh dear! I shall be late; I know I'll miss Mr. Croft. Olga,
does that darn show very much? (*She balances on one leg.*)

OLGA. It'll pass. (*She goes into kitchen* R.)

VERONICA. What's the time?

JESSIE. Just gone quarter to eight. (*Looks at* VIVIANNE *again.*)
Another cup?

VIVIANNE. No—no.

VERONICA. I know I'll never make it. (*She puts her cup on
table.*)

JESSIE. Well, why don't you get a move on, instead of talkin'
about it?

VERONICA. Kiss Elaine goodbye for me. (*Exit* L. *with a lot of
fuss and flurry.*)

VIVIANNE (*stirs restlessly on her chair—to* CHRISTINE). Is there any news?

CHRISTINE (*folding the letter*). Yes—he's coming home in August—only another two months. (*She is curbing her happiness—smiling in spite of herself.*) He may have to go back to America permanently, but he'll be taking us with him, of course.

JESSIE. Some folks have all the luck. Hey, Chris, do you know you've missed your bus?

CHRISTINE. It doesn't matter—I don't think I'll go to work to-day. I'll ring up the shop and tell them I'm not well. Maybe I'll take Christopher out somewhere.

JESSIE. I suppose you wouldn't like to take the lot of them? I met a smashing chap at the dance last night—commercial traveller—wanted to take me to Southend in the car. I've been dying for a chance to wear my bikini. (*She wriggles voluptuously.*)

LAURA. I'll go and see if Sal's got Barbara ready. Could you help me get this trunk out in the hall?

JESSIE. Sure.

> (*They try to move the trunk, letting it fall with a clatter.* VIVIANNE *starts violently. Between them they go out with trunk* L., JESSIE *returning almost at once.*)

VIVIANNE (*rises and crosses to the window—she stands looking out*). He knows it's going to be another lovely day—(*Turning to* CHRISTINE.)—or is it dark in there?

CHRISTINE. I—don't know, darling. (*She is* R. *of table and behind it.*)

> (HELEN *enters briskly,* L.)

HELEN. Why can't that stupid Olga do anything properly? I missed my morning——

> (OLGA *enters quickly* R.)

OLGA. Shut up.

HELEN. What?

OLGA. I said shut up; some folks have got more important things to worry about.

HELEN. Oh! I see. (*After a pause.*) Will you go and get those children dressed? They're making a terrible row in the nursery.

JESSIE. I'll go when I'm ready.

(LAURA *enters* L., *puts her head round the door.*)

LAURA. My taxi's here; I'm just going, Mrs. Allistair.

JESSIE. Aren't you goin' to see 'er off? (*As* HELEN *hesitates.*) Go on. (*Gives her a push towards the door, glancing over her shoulder at* VIVIANNE.)

LAURA. Come and say good-bye to Barbara.

(JESSIE, HELEN *and* LAURA *go out: their voices can be heard off. At the same time the clock begins to strike "eight". VIVIANNE *stands still, looking out of the window.*)

JESSIE (*off*). Wave to auntie.

(*As the clock is striking,* CHRISTINE *and* OLGA *are standing motionless, watching* VIVIANNE.)

VIVIANNE. I can still feel the sun. I can still see it shining . . . *Breaks off into agonised sobbing as*

THE CURTAIN FALLS

ACT II

SCENE 2

The same, two months later.

The room is in its usual state of disorder—CHRISTOPHER'S cradle has been placed R. of the bed occupied by VIVIANNE.

When the curtain rises, VIVIANNE is lying on her bed. She is dressed rather carelessly and, although her manner is less strained than in the earlier scenes, there is a weary hopelessness about her. One feels she is more closely associated with her surroundings than she has been before. OLGA is standing in front of the mirror making up: she is over-smartly dressed to go out.

VIVIANNE (*sits up, leaning forward to look into the cot*). I'm worried about Christopher. I really think we should have called a doctor.

OLGA. You know damn well Nellie won't have one inside the house. Don't worry, honey, Chris can take him to the clinic to-morrow.

VIVIANNE. I'm so glad she's coming home to-night—it's been an awful week—Jess is never in and Sal's so *stupid*.

OLGA. I don't envy you stuck in this joint all day: you know something, kid? The only thing that makes life bearable for girls like us is money. Have you noticed the difference in my kid since I packed up the shop and started bringing in the necessary? She's put on weight already. (*After a pause, turning to her.*) It's just occurred to me, I don't see why I should keep on tipping Jess when you do all the dirty work. Supposing I was to slip you an extra ten bob a week?

VIVIANNE. No, thanks—it isn't necessary.

OLGA. Don't take offence—I know you do your best for all of them, but it's a pretty thankless job looking after other people's brats. (*She picks up her handbag from table c., then sits in chair L. of it.*)

VIVIANNE. One job's as good as another, as far as I'm concerned. Wonder what time Chris will get in—the Brighton shop closes at five and it's after eight o'clock. I hope she's had a meal, the larder's just about cleared out.

OLGA. Oh, she'll have eaten down town. You don't want to worry yourself so much about these girls. The more you do in a place like this the more they expect. (*Turns, looking at her sympathetically.*) You look pretty tired.

VIVIANNE (*nods—pushing back her hair*). I get tired these days; I suppose it's only natural.

OLGA. That lazy bitch Jess is taking advantage. Just because you're here she figures it's all right to take a holiday.

VIVIANNE. I don't mind working. It gives you less time to think: it's Christopher that's worrying me. He just lies there and sleeps. It isn't like him. If only Helen would let me call the doctor.

OLGA. Has she seen the kid?

VIVIANNE (*nods*). She says it's nothing. What am I to do?— She ought to know more about babies than I do.

OLGA. Maybe it's all right. They do act rather alarming sometimes.

VIVIANNE. Christopher isn't acting alarming. He's just lying still and quiet.

OLGA. Look, honey, if you fly into a panic every time one of the kids has a tummy ache you'll be a nervous wreck before you leave here.

VIVIANNE (*bitterly with a laugh*). Before I leave.

OLGA. Well you're not figuring on stopping here for ever, are you?

VIVIANNE. I don't know. I haven't thought about the future. I stopped thinking about it when Johnny died.

OLGA (*rises and sits on the bed beside her*). Listen, how's this for an idea? I've been working on it for some time: I've got a room in Soho, see? It's not a very grand room but it's all right. Supposing after you had your kid you came and shared with me? Between the two of us we could rake in enough money to have the kids looked after properly—you know, send them to a nursery school. Nellie will keep 'em till they're old enough and Jess'll see they're treated right if we make it worth her while.

VIVIANNE (*doubtfully*). I don't know, Olga.

OLGA. You mean you don't approve—eh? What sort of a life did you live before your Johnny came along? Don't try to tell me you were another Veronica.

VIVIANNE. It doesn't seem as though I lived at all—before Johnny.

OLGA. Oh! come off it. No man on earth is so wonderful as all that.

VIVIANNE. He wasn't wonderful. He wasn't any good. He didn't even love me. Don't tell me! I'm a fool—I threw my life away and I'm not even regretting.

(OLGA *nods thoughtfully.* VIVIANNE *smiles suddenly; rises, patting her on the shoulder; moves cradle about two feet away from the divan and crosses to table* C.)

(*After a pause.*) Thank you, Olga, it was nice of you to think about me and when I get things straightened out I'll consider your proposition seriously.

OLGA (*rising*). You might as well. What else is there for girls like us?

(VERONICA *enters* L.)

VERONICA (*to* OLGA). Are you going out?

OLGA. I am. (*She goes to table for her handbag.*)

VERONICA. Where?

OLGA. Down town.

VERONICA. May I come with you? I'm so *bored* with sitting in here.

OLGA. You may not. (*She crosses* VERONICA *and takes down her coat from the back of the door* L.)

VERONICA. Why not? I hate going anywhere alone. Perhaps we could go to the pictures.

OLGA. Sorry—I've got other plans.

VERONICA. A date?

OLGA. Not exactly!

VERONICA. Then why can't I come, too? Where are you going?

OLGA (*turning in doorway*). I'm going to feed the pigeons in Trafalgar Square!

VERONICA (*slumps into a chair* L. *of table glaring at* OLGA *spitefully*). You might be interested to know your little girl's yelling her head off.

OLGA. Oh, damn! Isn't Sally in the nursery?

VERONICA. No—she's getting Mrs. Allistair's supper.

       (OLGA *looks appealingly at* VIVIANNE.)

VIVIANNE. I'm sorry—but I'd rather not leave Christopher and Helen doesn't want him with the others, just in *case* he's sickening for anything.

OLGA. Okay, you sit down and relax. You look as if you'd done enough for one day. (*Exit* L.)

       (VIVIANNE *sits in chair above table.*)

VERONICA (*with a long sigh*). Oh dear!

VIVIANNE. What's the matter?

VERONICA. I'm so sick of rushing home every night to put Elaine to bed. That's all I ever do—just put Elaine to bed and sit here listening to a lot of women swearing at each other. I might as well be old and ugly.

VIVIANNE. You're young enough to make something out of your life.

VERONICA. How can I when I have to live like this? Mr. Croft was going to take me out to dinner to-night but I couldn't go as I was. He wanted to drive me home and wait while I changed, but I'd have died rather than let him come here.

VIVIANNE. Perhaps he can suggest something better.

VERONICA (*after a pause*). He has.

VIVIANNE. Are you going to be a little fool? He's married, isn't he?

VERONICA (*going to fireplace*). He's been kind to me—and nothing could be worse than this. Of course we'd have to be discreet. It would be fatal if anyone knew at the office.

VIVIANNE. It would be fatal all right. The novelty would soon wear off and before you knew it you would find yourself minus your little love nest and your job. For heaven's sake be sensible, child, or you'll land yourself in another mess. One of these days some nice young man will turn up who'll be fool enough to marry you.

VERONICA (*turning tearfully*). What *nice* young man would ever marry me?

VIVIANNE. They're the only sort who would. You'd be most unsatisfactory as a mistress.

VERONICA. (*drying her eyes*). Why?

VIVIANNE. Leave that sort of thing to the Olgas of this world. They'd never make a whore of you in a million years; so just dry your tears and make up your mind to be patient.

VERONICA (*puzzled*). But I am, aren't I?

VIVIANNE. You are what?

VERONICA. A—what you said.

VIVIANNE (*laughing*). Certainly not! You haven't the most elementary qualifications. You wait. You'll marry some respectable young man who'll set you up in a semi-detached villa, and all this will be written off as experience.

VERONICA. You really think so?

VIVIANNE. I'm sure of it.

VERONICA (*moving slowly to chair R. of table*). You'd hate it, wouldn't you? I mean a life like that. Oh! yes, I've seen the way you and Olga laugh at me behind my back. You think it's awful to be ordinary and respectable. I used to think so, too. I wanted to do something desperate and disgraceful just to show my mother and father that I didn't care a damn. I thought it would be wonderful to have a job in London and live away from home. (*After a pause, with an effort.*) It all turned out so different from what I expected.

If I'd stopped at home I'd have married someone, like you said, and had a little house and looked after my baby. All my friends would have come round to see her and said how cute she was. (*Breaks off suddenly, near to tears.*) I don't really want to go and live with Mr. Croft——

(*She sinks into chair* R. *of table, burying her head in her hands and gives way to her tears. After a pause* VIVIANNE *rises and touches her shoulder gently.*)

VIVIANNE. I'm not laughing. Maybe we all wanted something like that, but we wanted other things as well, and nobody can have it all. It's all according to the people we love and the sort of breaks we get. When you came here, you were just a silly, frightened little girl, trying to kid yourself that you hadn't made a mess of things. If we laughed at you it was only because your bluffing didn't fool us. Now you're old enough to face up to the facts.

VERONICA (*looking at her*). I never heard you talk like that before. I didn't think you minded what happened to any-one.

VIVIANNE. I only don't mind what happens to *me* any more.

VERONICA. I was scared of you when I first came here; after all the things I'd read about you in the papers. I'd never met anyone who was mixed up in a murder case before.

VIVIANNE (*turning away, half amused*). Oh God!

VERONICA (*hastily*). I'm sorry, I suppose I shouldn't talk about it.

VIVIANNE. It doesn't matter. (*Crosses back to the cradle* L. *and stands staring into it.*)

VERONICA. Have I upset you?

VIVIANNE. Hush! He's waking. (*Leans suddenly over the cot, her voice gentle and anxious.*) What's the matter, honey? (*With a sigh.*) I wish your mummy would come home!

VERONICA (*crossing to* R. *of cot*). Is he very sick?

VIVIANNE. I hope not.

VERONICA. Why didn't you ring up the doctor while Nellie wasn't around? Once he was here she couldn't very well send him away.

VIVIANNE. The phone's still out of order.

VERONICA. Couldn't you have taken him to the clinic?

VIVIANNE (*wearily*). Do you think he'd drink a little milk now? He hasn't had a thing all day.

VERONICA (*as* VIVIANNE *turns towards kitchen—stops her*). I'll get it. (*Exit* R.)

VIVIANNE. Would you? Thanks.

(*Sits on bed still watching the child in the cradle* R. CHRISTINE *enters* L. *She looks well and very smart, and carries a light suitcase which she sets down with a sigh of relief.*)

CHRISTINE. Home at last! Did you think I'd run away?

VIVIANNE. You look well—quite brown too. Shouldn't think they've overworked you.

CHRISTINE. Oh, I did my share—but the shop shut at five and the evenings were glorious. What's Christopher doing down here?

VIVIANNE (*rising hastily*). Don't wake him; I brought him down to keep me company.

CHRISTINE (*amused*). Don't you get enough of babies, with that brood to look after all day?

VIVIANNE. Have you had a meal?

CHRISTINE. Yes, thanks. (*Removes her hat and gloves, puts them on dresser up* L. *then crosses to* R. *of cradle.*)

VIVIANNE (*urgently*). I've only just managed to get him off to sleep.

CHRISTINE. Sit down and tell me all the news.

VIVIANNE (*sitting on divan*). There isn't any.

CHRISTINE. Good, then I can tell you mine. I feel I want to shout it from the roof tops.

VIVIANNE. Ron? (*As* CHRISTINE *nods eagerly.*) I thought it might be.

CHRISTINE. Next week, Viv. He's coming home next week. I still can't quite believe it, though I've read his letter at least a dozen times.

VIVIANNE. Of course I'm awfully pleased. I suppose you'll be leaving here almost at once?

CHRISTINE. We'll have to go to an hotel. It'll cost a lot, but what else can we do? Anyway, something will turn up. How have you been keeping, pet? You're looking rather wan. I hope you've not been overdoing it.

VIVIANNE. Tired, that's all.

CHRISTINE (sitting in chair L. of table.) Only a few weeks more, then you'll be going into the country. Think how lovely it will be getting away from this room.

VIVIANNE (abruptly). You forget I'm coming back.

CHRISTINE. I know, dear, but it won't be for long. Once you've got over the baby you'll feel like coping again.

VIVIANNE. I've already received a perfectly charming proposition from Olga which will probably be the answer to all my problems.

CHRISTINE. What do you mean?

VIVIANNE (imitating OLGA). As she says, "there's not much else fer girls like us". (Laughs.) You're almost as easily shocked as Veronica.

CHRISTINE. You wouldn't live like that, Viv, I know you wouldn't.

VIVIANNE. It's a matter of supreme indifference to me how I live. I've lost everything and from now on I intend to remain with nothing to lose.

CHRISTINE. You're not like that really. I've watched you in the last few weeks with those children.

VIVIANNE. Young children are like animals. You've got to treat them decently unless you're completely inhuman.

CHRISTINE. You didn't have to bring him down to keep you company. (Rises and moves to the cradle.)

VIVIANNE (rising). Chris!

CHRISTINE (*without turning*). Yes?

VIVIANNE. Maybe I should have told you right away but I didn't want to frighten you.

> (*Breaks off as* VERONICA *enters* R. *with the milk.*)

VERONICA. Here you are. Shall we give it him now?

VIVIANNE. Wait a minute.

> (*Looks worriedly at* VERONICA *who pauses, watching* CHRISTINE. HELEN *enters* L., *comes forward briskly.*)

HELEN. Ah, my dear. I wondered when you were coming home. Did you have a good time in Brighton?

CHRISTINE (*turning to her*). I didn't go there to have a good time—I went there to work.

HELEN. Yes, but I know what you girls are for combining business with pleasure.

CHRISTINE (*raising her eyebrows*). Do you? Well it was what I suppose you'd call a last fling. Ron's coming home on Tuesday.

HELEN. You've been very lucky—luckier than most.

VERONICA (*on* HELEN'S R.). Shouldn't we give it him, Viv, before it gets cold?

CHRISTINE (*turning to* VERONICA). What? You're not going to wake him up to give him milk?

HELEN. I shouldn't bother. He's been off his food to-day, but it probably won't do him any harm to go without it.

CHRISTINE. Is he ill? (*She bends anxiously over the cradle.*)

HELEN. Not ill, my dear; just a little out of sorts.

CHRISTINE (*sharply to* VIVIANNE). Why didn't you tell me?

VIVIANNE. I was just going to tell you. Mrs. Allistair says it's nothing serious.

HELEN. Of course it isn't.

> (*As* CHRISTINE *kneels by cradle.*)

I shouldn't disturb him. It will do him good to sleep.

CHRISTINE (*alarmed*). He isn't sleeping.

HELEN. Only because you've just woken him up.

W.T.—E

CHRISTINE. His eyes are open. Look at him. He doesn't know me.

HELEN. The poor little thing isn't properly awake yet.

VIVIANNE. No, he's been like that all day. I was sure it wasn't natural. That's why I wanted to call a doctor.

CHRISTINE (*furiously*). Why didn't you? (*To* VIVIANNE.) You promised you'd take care of him. I thought I could rely on you.

VIVIANNE. Chris—I'm sorry—but Mrs. Allistair said——

CHRISTINE. You've got eyes, haven't you? Couldn't you see for yourself? (*To* HELEN.) I'm going to call the doctor in at once. (*Rising.*)

HELEN. I should leave it till to-morrow—besides, the phone's out of order.

CHRISTINE. Wait till to-morrow! He could be dead by then. (*Pushes her aside, grabbing her bag from the table.*)

VERONICA (*going to* CHRISTINE). I'll go, if you like. It won't take me a moment.

CHRISTINE. Go to Dr. Brandon at the end of the road, and make him understand it's urgent. He should have been called hours ago.

(VERONICA *takes her coat from the door.*)

HELEN (*looking into the cradle*). He certainly looks a little . . . (*Turning to* VIVIANNE.) You never told me he was in a coma.

VIVIANNE (*distressed*). That's not true . . .

HELEN (*interrupting*). When I looked at him he was sleeping naturally. Can't you tell the difference? I put him in your care. I naturally assumed you would call me if there was any change.

VIVIANNE. But you saw him half an hour ago.

HELEN. There is no use arguing, the damage is done now.

VIVIANNE. Chris—you believe me?

CHRISTINE. Hurry up, Veronica.

VERONICA. I'll run both ways. (*Exit* L.)

VIVIANNE. You must believe me.

CHRISTINE. Of course I believe you. I hope she'll hurry. (*She kneels at the upstage end of cradle, between* HELEN *and* VIVIANNE.)

HELEN (*to* VIVIANNE). Don't reproach yourself too much. Christine realises you've not been feeling very well. She'll make allowances.

VIVIANNE. That had nothing to do with it at all. You wouldn't *let* me call a doctor.

HELEN. Have I to keep on telling you that when I looked at him it wasn't necessary? If you felt so worried, why didn't you do something about it?

VIVIANNE. You know perfectly well that I . . .

CHRISTINE. For heaven's sake be quiet.

HELEN (*going to door* L.). I'd better run up to the nursery and make sure the others are all right. If the doctor thinks it's anything infectious he may want to have a look at them. (*She turns.*) Don't worry, Vivianne, if there's any question of negligence I'll put a word in for you.

VIVIANNE (*bitterly*). So that's the way you're going to work it.

(*Exit* HELEN L. CHRISTINE *picks up baby and moves* R.)

Listen, darling. I was going to take him to the clinic. I had put him in the pram and got my hat and coat ready to go when suddenly I felt most awfully giddy and I had to lie down for a bit. When Olga came in she gave me some brandy and I felt heaps better, but it was too late to take him by that time.

CHRISTINE (*her back to* VIVIANNE). I shouldn't have left him.

VIVIANNE. You couldn't have stopped him being ill, Chris.

CHRISTINE (*puts the child carefully back in the cot and covers him up*). I would have known at once if there was anything wrong with him.

(*Turns with sudden penitence, as* VIVIANNE *sits down on her own bed and begins to cry, wearily making an effort to stifle her sobs.*)

Vivianne—don't—I'm sorry. I didn't mean to fly at you. I was so worried.

VIVIANNE. It doesn't matter what anybody else thinks. Helen can shift the blame on to me, but I really did look after him. Ask Olga. I was sitting up all night.

CHRISTINE (*crossing to her, puts an arm round her shoulders*). Yes, lamb, I know. You mustn't cry. You're tired out.

VIVIANNE (*struggling to control her tears, pats* CHRISTINE'S *hand*). He'll be all right.

CHRISTINE. He's got to be. If he's not, I'll kill her.

VIVIANNE. You ... (*Rises.*) Shall we try to give him the milk?

CHRISTINE (*shakes her head slowly*). He wouldn't take it. I wonder how long Veronica will be?

VIVIANNE. It shouldn't take her long. (*Looks round hurriedly.*) I ought to tidy this place up if the doctor's coming.

CHRISTINE (*a new, hard note in her voice*). Leave it as it is; we're not having any more of that. They're not dealing with Rosie, this time.

VIVIANNE. Helen will only say that I've not done my job.

CHRISTINE. Don't be such a fool. You've been working practically all day. Who cooked the meals and did the shopping?

VIVIANNE. I know what she's like. She's so damnably clever.

CHRISTINE. It won't help to have you taken ill as well. (*Glances round and sees small flask on the table. She pours a little into a glass and passes it to* VIVIANNE.) Here, finish it up.

　　　(CHRISTINE *puts flask on top of cupboard* L. *as* VIVIANNE *drinks obediently.* VERONICA *enters breathless from* L.) Well?

VERONICA. He wasn't in—a case. He might be back in an hour or two.

CHRISTINE. An hour! I'll have to go for someone else. You left a message, didn't you? (*Goes to table for her handbag.*)

VERONICA. Yes—but his housekeeper seemed a bit vague. I think he's out at a confinement.

CHRISTINE. Oh God!

VERONICA. There's another doctor on the Hampstead Road—
I'll go there if you like.

CHRISTINE. No, I'll go. I've got to bring him back with me.
(*Looks undecidedly at the cot—then lifts the child out gently,
turning to* VIVIANNE.) Viv.

VIVIANNE. Yes, Chris?

CHRISTINE. Will you promise not to leave him for a moment?
You understand? Hold him till I get back. Don't let anybody take him from you.

VIVIANNE. Yes—but Helen. She knows more about babies
than I do.

CHRISTINE. Helen mustn't touch him. He's afraid of Helen. I
don't want him to wake up and be frightened. Promise me?

VIVIANNE. Yes, Chris.

(CHRISTINE *puts the child in* VIVIANNE'S *arms.* VIVI-
ANNE *takes him dazedly, holding him against her.*)

CHRISTINE. Just sit and hold him—I won't be long.

VIVIANNE (*crying*). Yes.

CHRISTINE. He's going to be all right. You stay here too,
Veronica, in case there's anything she needs.

VERONICA. Oh yes, I will.

(CHRISTINE *looks at her child—hesitating for an instant,
then goes out hurriedly* L.)

VERONICA (*helpfully*). Don't worry—I expect he'll get better.
(*She moves to divan* L.)

VIVIANNE. I think he's dying.

VERONICA (*sitting*). Oh, no! (*After a pause.*) He looks so little
to die.

VIVIANNE. I wish it could be my baby instead. (*Sits silently for
a moment looking down at the child. Almost in a whisper.*) If my
baby could die at this moment and Christopher live.

VERONICA. Lots of children are ill, but they get better: Rosie's
Alfie did.

VIVIANNE. He wasn't ill like this. (*With horror in her voice.*)
Look at him! Where's Christine? Go after her.

VERONICA. She'll soon be back.

VIVIANNE (*hopelessly*). It's no good.

(VERONICA *watches her, alarmed. She rises.*)

VERONICA (*doubtfully*). I'll get Mrs. Allistair.

(*She runs out* L. *calling* MRS. ALLISTAIR *in frightened voice. Almost at once* HELEN *enters followed by* OLGA *and* VERONICA.)

HELEN. What is it?

VERONICA. I think he's worse.

OLGA. What the devil?

(HELEN *looks at the child but* VIVIANNE *holds him away from her.*)

HELEN. I'm afraid we're going to be too late to save him.

OLGA (*coming down to* L. *side of divan*). What do you mean? It's not as bad as that! You said this afternoon . . .

HELEN. I was given to understand the child was sleeping. If only Vivianne had been discerning enough to realise he was in a coma, we might have done something about it.

OLGA. Why, you filthy rotten liar!

VIVIANNE. It wasn't my fault——

HELEN. Let me take him.

VIVIANNE. No. (*She rises and crosses to divan* D.R.)

HELEN. Give him to me, you little fool! Can't you see? He's going.

VIVIANNE. No, no! Christine said I'd got to hold him—I won't let Christine's baby die. (*She sits on* L. *end of divan, hugging the child to her protectingly.*)

(VERONICA *has moved round to sit on* R. *end of the divan.*)

HELEN. If you feel so strongly about it, you might have taken him to the clinic this afternoon.

OLGA. She wasn't well. When I got in, she could hardly get up off that bed.

HELEN (*turning to* OLGA). It's the first I've heard of it. Why didn't you call me?

OLGA. You'd only have made her feel worse.

HELEN. She must have recovered very quickly.

OLGA. I gave her some brandy. (*Picks up the flask from cupboard* L.) My God! Has Jess been in?

HELEN. She has not. (*Eyeing the flask.*) It certainly seems as though somebody's made short work of it. It wouldn't surprise me if she couldn't call me when the child got worse because she wasn't sober enough.

OLGA. I've known some pretty lousy characters, but you're just about the end.

VIVIANNE (*sharply*). Hush.

(*They both look at her—she seems suddenly to relax, holding the child more naturally.*)

It's all right. I think he's sleeping now—really sleeping. He seems quite peaceful.

(HELEN *crosses and looks over her shoulder—lifting the shawl to look at the child's face. She touches him with her finger, then straightens slowly.*)

HELEN. You can put him back in the cot now, Vivianne, he's dead.

OLGA. What?

VERONICA. No. (*She rises.*)

(HELEN *holds out her arms for the baby, but* VIVIANNE *does not seem to hear. She tries to take the child, but* VIVIANNE *starts back violently, pushing her away.*)

VIVIANNE. No! I promised Chris.

HELEN. Don't you understand what I said? He isn't breathing. You'd better give him to me.

VIVIANNE (*staring at her hopelessly*). You're lying. You want to take him away from me.

(*As nobody answers.*)

If he was dead, he'd be cold. He isn't cold—he's warm.

(HELEN *looks helplessly at* OLGA, *who comes to* VIVIANNE.)

Christine will be back soon with the doctor. He's only sleeping, isn't he?

HELEN. You mustn't blame yourself too much. Maybe they wouldn't have been able to save him anyway.

VERONICA (*sobbing suddenly*). He's so *small*.

HELEN. Shut up.

OLGA (*gently*). Look honey, your arms must be aching. Supposing you give him to me? Chris wouldn't mind me holding him. (*She kneels by* VIVIANNE.)

VIVIANNE. I promised her I'd keep him in my arms.

OLGA (*rising, and turning furiously on* HELEN). This is all your fault! Well, you needn't think you'll get away with it this time. Chris knows who's word to take. She'll tell the doctor everything.

HELEN. I don't think she will.

OLGA. Listen. You might have pulled a fast one on Rosie; but this time you're dealing with a different kind of girl.

HELEN. It's my word against Vivianne's, of course. Christine can believe whichever she pleases — but the authorities might not be quite so easy to convince.

OLGA. You're so clever, aren't you?

HELEN. I think, when she reviews the situation calmly, she'll decide to pass it over as quietly as possible. Vivianne has had to face enough unfavourable publicity already—probably quite as much as she can stand.

OLGA (*with hatred*). But one of these days you'll come up with someone as wicked as you are—someone who'll risk their lot to see you dragged through the mud. *Then* you'll have to pay. (*With so much venom in her voice that* HELEN *turns from her glance uncertainly.*

VERONICA *continues to sob monotonously;* VIVIANNE *continues to hold the baby closely, cradling him in her arms as if he were alive, as* OLGA *turns to her.*)

Better let me take him, honey. There's nothing else we can do.

CURTAIN

ACT III

SCENE I

The same four days later. The table has been moved slightly farther downstage c.

MOLLY, *a soft-voiced, rather pretty Irish girl, is sitting by the fireplace knitting.* VIVIANNE *is lying on her bed* L. *She wears a loose dressing gown and her hair is tangled and uncombed. She stares morosely at the ceiling, her hands playing nervously with the blankets.*

MOLLY. It's almost time I was off. I have to be at the café by seven. Would you know what times the buses run to Leicester Square?

(*After a pause, as* VIVIANNE *does not reply.*)

It wouldn't worry me working evenings if it wasn't for walking home alone so late at night. You read of such terrible things—hold-ups and murders and all the rest of it.

(*Hurriedly—still receiving no response.*)

Is there anything I can do for you before I go?

VIVIANNE. No, thanks.

MOLLY. It must be terribly boring with nobody to talk to. Jess is going to the fair and Olga says she is on the night shift, though I didn't know the factories opened August Monday. Couldn't you do a bit of knittin'? You'll be wantin' things for the baby, and there isn't much time.

VIVIANNE. I don't know how to knit.

MOLLY. Then will I be showin' you?

VIVIANNE. You certainly won't.

MOLLY (*after a pause*). Well, anyway, Sally isn't going to the fair: she'll be able to get you your supper. There's a nice bit of beef left from yesterday and some salad.

VIVIANNE. I shan't want anything and if I do I can get it.

MOLLY (*rising, and looking in mirror above mantelpiece*). Mrs.
Allistair said you weren't to go walkin' around. I guess she
feels there's been enough trouble in the last few days with
that poor little boy goin'—God rest his soul. Mrs. Allistair
was terribly upset. There were tears in her eyes when she
told me. She's a wonderful woman; the sisters at the convent told me she never spares herself.

(*As* VIVIANNE *laughs shortly.*)

She says she's arranging for you to go to the country sooner
than you'd planned. It will give you a chance to get your
strength back before the baby comes.

VIVIANNE. You mean it will keep me out of the way till all this
fuss about Christopher is over.

MOLLY. It wasn't your fault. Mrs. Allistair told me so herself.
" The poor girl was sick," she said. " If only she'd had the
sense to admit it instead of being brave and trying to carry
on." Will your friend be comin' back here, now the funeral's
over?

VIVIANNE. No—Chris won't come back.

MOLLY. Poor thing—but it's the will of God.

VIVIANNE. The will of God. (*Her voice rises with such contempt
and bitterness that* MOLLY *turns round, startled.*) The will of
God.

(JESSIE *enters in a black, chiffon, off-the-shoulder blouse and
a very short, coloured skirt. She pushes* MOLLY *aside to get to
the mirror.*)

JESSIE. Out of the way. Got a date with a smashin' chap at
Jack Straw's Castle—six o'clock. I've told Nellie she needn't
expect me back until she sees me. I'm goin' back with 'im
to cook 'is supper after. 'e's got a " pressher " cooker.

MOLLY. Has he?

JESSIE. That's what 'e tells me, but you never can tell until you
get there, can you? Does this blouse look all right? (*She
crosses* C. *below divan and turns round for* VIVIANNE'S *approval.*)

MOLLY. Have you got it on the right way round?

JESSIE.   Course I 'ave, you soppy date.   'ere, Viv—you're sure it don't make me look common? This chap likes a bit of class.

VIVIANNE (*impatiently, her head averted*). No—no! It's perfectly all right.

JESSIE. Don't bother to *look*, will you?

VIVIANNE. I've told you, it's all right.

JESSIE (*pushing her blouse even further off one shoulder*). There we are then—all set for action.

(*Turns as* SAL *enters.*)

Just off, ducks. Be a good girl, and I'll bring you back a toffee apple.

SAL. I want to go to the fair—you went Sat'day night.

JESSIE (*crossing to door* L.). Now don't be soft. You know very well you promised to stop and mind the kids. What you grumbling about? I'm givin' you a couple of bob so as you can take yourself to the Odeon to-morrow, aren't I?

SAL (*obstinately*). I want to go to the fair and ride on the roundabouts.

JESSIE (*crossly*). Well you can't. Cheerio, girls. If I don't get back to-night you'll know what's cookin'. (*Exit* L.)

SAL (*tearfully*). Nellie said I could go this time—Jessie always goes.

MOLLY (*putting her knitting-bag on table*). Never mind. You stop and talk to Viv. She can't go to the fair either.

VIVIANNE. You're going to be late.

MOLLY. I must fly. You're sure you're going to be all right?

VIVIANNE. Yes—I'm fine.

MOLLY. Don't go trying to walk about or you might turn faint again. Mrs. Allistair doesn't think you ought to have gone to the funeral.

VIVIANNE. I'm perfectly all right, I tell you. For heaven's sake go to your café and leave me in peace.

MOLLY (*a little hurt*). I'm sure I've no wish to offend you.

VIVIANNE. You mustn't pay any attention to anything I say. Try to understand it's nothing personal.

MOLLY. Sure, you don't have to explain to me.

(*Pats* VIVIANNE's *hand kindly and fusses round the bed, raising the pillows with good-natured roughness.* VIVIANNE *acknowledges her unwelcome attention with a forced smile, then settles back, closing her eyes determinedly.*)

That's better: try and get a little sleep. I'll be back about twelve, but I'll come in very quietly. Veronica's gone home for the week-end, so there'll be no one to disturb you.

VIVIANNE. Yes, I'll try to sleep. Good night, Molly.

MOLLY. Good night, me dear. Good night, Sal. (*Exit* L.)

(SAL *crosses to bed and stands looking down at* VIVIANNE, *who keeps her eyes closed for a moment. Then, aware that she is being watched, she opens them and speaks with exasperation.*)

VIVIANNE. Why don't you go upstairs?

SAL. I don't want to. They always leave me on my own. Won't they let you go to the fair, either?

VIVIANNE. I didn't want to go. If you must stay here sit down like a good girl and be quiet.

SAL. Nobody ever talks to me—only the babies. (*She sits in chair* L. *of table. A pause.*) There's an empty cot in the nursery. Are they going to put your baby in there, when it comes?

VIVIANNE. I don't know, Sally—perhaps.

SAL. Christopher's gone away. They put him in a box and took him away in a motor.

VIVIANNE (*closing her eyes again—painfully*). Yes.

SAL. Christine was crying. Was it because they took 'im away? I didn't let them take my baby away. We put 'im in the garden, where 'e could hear the other children playing. 'e didn't have no box to sleep in.

VIVIANNE (*with her eyes closed—not listening properly*). No.

SAL. Nellie said 'e'd like it better in the garden under the trees.

We didn't think 'e'd want to be alone. It was a secret. You won't tell anybody I told you?

VIVIANNE (*raising herself resignedly*). What did you say?

SAL. You won't tell anyone how we buried Frankie in the garden?

VIVIANNE. Who was Frankie?

SAL (*smiling to herself*). Frankie was my little boy.

VIVIANNE. You shouldn't say that. Don't you know it's wrong to make up stories?

SAL. I didn't make it up. Frankie and me was here before the others came.

VIVIANNE. You know you never had a little boy.

SAL. Yes I did. I 'ad a little baby of my own.

VIVIANNE. It's all right talking like that to me but other people may not understand.

SAL (*rising with a sly smile*). The others think I'm potty. They think I don't know nothin' about how babies come—but I know all about it. It's a secret between Nellie Allistair and me. (*She wanders over* R.)

(VIVIANNE *sits up, suddenly alert, propping herself on her elbow.*)

VIVIANNE. Tell me some more about Frankie, Sally. What did you say just now about putting him in the garden? Was he sick like Christopher; did the doctor come?

SAL. Oh no, Frankie wasn't sick—but 'is legs was crooked and he kept on fallin' down. 'e was a *naughty* baby. Nellie said if I didn't learn 'im to be clean she'd send 'im away.

VIVIANNE (*regarding her thoughtfully*). Did you have your baby in the hospital, Sal?

SAL. Oh no, Nellie took me to the country. There was a nice little cottage with a straw roof and chickens in the garden. You're goin' to the country, aren't you? (*She moves back towards* VIVIANNE.)

VIVIANNE. And after you had the baby you came back here?

(*She pulls* SAL *down so that she is kneeling by divan.*)

SAL. Yes, the lady brought me back. Afterwards she sent us lots more babies, but none of 'em stopped for long—only my Frankie.

VIVIANNE. How long was Frankie with you?

SAL. I dunno. 'e was big enough to walk if 'is legs would 'ave 'eld 'im. 'e was always fallin' down, but one day Nellie 'it 'im with a stick and 'e just lay there on the carpet. I wanted to put 'im to bed in the attic, but Nellie said it weren't no use, 'cos he was dead. (*After a pause, tearfully.*) 'e was a lovely baby. I didn't want to 'ide him in the garden but Nellie made me. She said girls like me didn't ought to 'ave babies and if they found out they'd put me in prison.

VIVIANNE. Sally, how long ago did it happen—three—four years?

(SAL *nods, snivelling.*)

And those other babies that came—how long did they used to stay?

SAL. Till the ladies came and took 'em.

VIVIANNE. What ladies? Their mothers?

SAL. No—nice ladies who 'adn't any little babies of their own. (*Frightened.*) But Nellie told me not to tell. She'd 'it me if she knew. You won't tell 'er, will you?

VIVIANNE. Of course I won't. Listen, Sally, if a policeman came to see you, would you tell him what you've just told me and show him whereabouts in the garden you put Frankie to sleep?

SAL. No—no—I don't like policemen. They'd take me to prison. (*Trying to rise, but* VIVIANNE *is holding her wrist.*)

VIVIANNE. No, they wouldn't—not if you told them the truth.

SAL. Nellie'd 'it me. I know she would. She said if I did let on she'd beat me with a stick.

VIVIANNE. We wouldn't let her. Be a good girl. I'll give you some chocolates that Christine had in a parcel from America —and you needn't share them with Jess. That can be a secret too. (*Impatiently, as* SALLY *continues to whimper.*) All right,

you stupid girl! I don't believe a word of it. I don't believe
you ever had a baby: you just made the whole thing up.

SAL. No, I didn't! Frankie's out there in the garden under that
big tree. (*She points out of the window then stares, still sniffing,
at* VIVIANNE *as she gets out of bed.*)
What you doin'?

VIVIANNE. I'm going out.

SAL. You're not goin' to call a policeman?

VIVIANNE (*grimly—looking for her shoes*). You go up to your
room and wait till I get back.

SAL (*screaming*). She'll 'it me. She'll 'it me.

VIVIANNE. So will I, if you don't stop making that noise.

SAL (*backing away from* VIVIANNE). No, you ain't goin' to call
a policeman. 'e'll lock me up.

(*Yells out in terror as* VIVIANNE *pushes her out of the way.*
HELEN *enters* L. *She stands very quietly in the doorway looking
steadily at* VIVIANNE. *There is no sound of her approach so
that it's impossible to say how long she might have been listening.* VIVIANNE *drops her coat which she was putting on and*
SAL *cringes away, shocked into silence.*)

HELEN (*very quietly in a cold voice*). What's the matter?

SAL. I didn't tell 'er nothin'—I didn't.

HELEN. No? Go upstairs. (*Her voice is steady and dangerously
calm. As* SAL *does not reply.*) Go upstairs.

(SAL *slips past her and out* L., *sobbing loudly again.* HELEN
stands silently until she has gone, then she turns to VIVIANNE;
her voice and manner are absolutely normal. VIVIANNE *is* R. *of
her divan.*)
I thought we agreed that you should stay in bed? The tension of the last few days has taxed your strength more than
you realise, I'm afraid.

VIVIANNE. I'm feeling much stronger than I've felt for a very
long time.

HELEN (*coming down* L. *of table*). That's fine. Don't go and spoil
it by doing anything rash.

VIVIANNE. How long had you been listening outside that door?

HELEN. What makes you think I've been listening at all?

VIVIANNE. Let's not beat about the bush—you heard what Sal told me. I suppose no one would pay much attention to the ramblings of a poor, idiot girl.

HELEN. She has a confidential mood from time to time but, as you say, no one has been so foolish as to pay much attention to them.

VIVIANNE (*calmly*). What a pity.

HELEN. It would be a *pity* to go getting yourself involved in what didn't concern you when you've so many problems of your own. I told you that I'd arranged for my friend to take you some weeks earlier than she intended. You could go to the country next week. I'm sure you'll find the cottage very charming: a nice country holiday is exactly what you need.

VIVIANNE. Sorry, Helen—that sort of talk doesn't wash with me. (*She moves across* R. *away from* HELEN.)

HELEN. Interfering with my affairs can only defeat your purpose. I've been a good friend to you. Sal doesn't understand, but I was being a friend to her when I kept her baby's birth a secret. She was only fifteen and, as you know, mentally deficient. If they'd found out they'd have packed her straight off to a home.

VIVIANNE (*turning and speaking with low intensity*). How many other children have you brought into the world as furtively, and how many have died or been bartered like cattle? You've been very clever, Helen—very smart—but I'm not afraid of you. I've got nothing to fear and nothing to lose.

HELEN. If you bring all this to light I shan't be the only one who will have to suffer. You realise that, don't you? They'll thrash it out in Court and everything you've done—everything you've been—will be brought before the public eye again.

VIVIANNE. That might have mattered once, but not any more. You've destroyed any pride or self-respect I still hung on to.

HELEN. Have you forgotten about your child? What is this going to do to him? Be sensible. The public isn't interested in what happens to the sort of girls I take in. They don't want to know.

VIVIANNE (*centre-stage*). A lot of things go on that the public don't want to know. So they look the other way—the same as the Welfare people do when they come down here. They're not really fooled by the show you put on for them, but it's easier not to look too closely. I've seen so much dirt I'm just not squeamish any more. Get out of my way. (*She moves towards door* L.)

HELEN. I'm sorry for you, Vivianne; right from the beginning I've wished to help you, but you always lived too much inside yourself. Wouldn't it be better if we tried to understand each other?

VIVIANNE (*pushing her aside*). Can't you see when you're beaten? (*Makes another move to pass her but* HELEN *grabs her by the arm.*) Let go of me.

HELEN. Where are you going?

VIVIANNE. I'm going to the police.

HELEN. Oh no, you're not. Get back to bed before you do yourself some harm. (*She throws* VIVIANNE *on to her divan* L.)

VIVIANNE. Let me pass. (*She rises and tries to throw off* HELEN'S *hand.* HELEN *grasps her more firmly.*

VIVIANNE *struggles fiercely for a moment, then her resistance weakens.* HELEN *flings her away from her violently so that she staggers across the stage and falls against the end of the divan, down* R. *She half straightens up, then groans and collapses on to the floor.* HELEN *stands watching her, slightly upstage of her.*)

VIVIANNE (*lifting herself a little with a great effort*). You'll—have to—help me.

(*As* HELEN *does not answer.*)

W.T.—F

Don't you understand? You'll have to call the doctor this time.

HELEN (*calmly*). Will I?

VIVIANNE (*not understanding*). Yes—hurry, please—I can't— (*Breaks off, fighting for control.*)

HELEN (*smoothly, looking down at her*). It's very early yet. Sally won't come down here again and the other girls aren't likely to be home till after midnight: when I last saw you, you were resting in your bed. (*Musing with a faint smile.*) I suppose you must have got up to get yourself a drink—turned faint again—fell. I was upstairs in my room—of course, I didn't hear you.

VIVIANNE (*very faintly—unbelieving—in a whisper*). You couldn't.

HELEN (*after a pause*). Couldn't I?

> Pauses a moment as VIVIANNE *makes a last feeble effort to rise, then collapses with a moan.* HELEN *walks slowly to the door* U.L. *as*

THE CURTAIN FALLS

ACT III

SCENE 2

The same, three days later.

The room is scrupulously clean and in perfect order for the first time—clean table-cloth, etc. When the curtain rises the stage is empty. Almost at once CHRISTINE *enters* L. *She is in her outdoor clothes and looks round rather puzzled; presently she raises her voice and calls off* L.

CHRISTINE. Is anybody in?

(*There is no answer; she puts down her bag and gloves on the table and looks thoughtfully at* VIVIANNE'S *tidily made bed. She crosses to the kitchen and calls off again.*)

Viv—Sally.

(JESSIE *enters from* L.—*very flustered and short tempered— with a tray in her hands.*)

JESSIE. Oh, it's you.

CHRISTINE. Hullo, Jess. There doesn't seem to be anyone around, so I just walked in. Where is everybody?

JESSIE (*slamming down tray on table.*) Of course you 'aven't 'eard.

CHRISTINE (*coming* R. *of table*). Heard what?

JESSIE. About Viv. The place is all topsy-turvy with nurses and doctors bargin' in and out. It doesn't even smell like 'ome. (*Sniffs disapprovingly.*) It's more like a bloody 'ospital and that miserable old bitch upstairs bossin' everyone about and yellin' out for trays all day.

CHRISTINE. What happened to Viv?

JESSIE. She nearly kicked the bucket the other night. Olga found 'er on the floor when she got back from town. They think she must 'ave fallen. Anyway, she's 'ad the baby— lovely little girl.

CHRISTINE. You mean, she had it here?

JESSIE (*nods*). We only got the doctor in the nick of time. You'd 'ave thought Nellie would have 'ad 'er packed off to the 'ospital as soon as it was over, wouldn't you? Seein' she 'ad such a bad time, but no—instead of that, she lets them bring that bloody nurse in, can't think what's got into 'er. She 'as even put 'er in the guest room.

CHRISTINE. But Vivianne—is she all right?

JESSIE. Couldn't say, dear. You know what nurses are—never tell you nothing, and she won't let none of us in there—not even Nellie, the old cow. She hasn't been out of the house since Vivianne had the kid; not even for a breather.

CHRISTINE. She'll have to let me see her. She's in the guest room, did you say? (*She moves towards door* L.)

JESSIE. That's right—but I don't suppose she'll let you past the door. (*Takes up tray again.*) Now she's callin' out for tea again, and Nellie says I've got to 'umour 'er—and that soppy Sally's no more good than a kick in the pants. Will you 'ave a cuppa, now you're 'ere? The kettle's on.

CHRISTINE (*worriedly*). Thanks.

(*Exit* JESSIE *to kitchen.*)

Is Vivianne out of danger?

JESSIE (*off*). I wouldn't know—but Nellie seems to think it's bad. 'as Ron come back yet?

CHRISTINE. Yes, I left him at the hotel. I wanted Vivianne to meet him.

(*As* JESSIE *enters* R. *with the teapot.*)

Are you taking that upstairs?

JESSIE (*grimly*). I am—and may it choke 'er. (*Pours a cup of tea for* CHRISTINE *and stands it* R. *of the table.*)

CHRISTINE. Perhaps you'll tell her there's a friend of Vivianne's waiting.

JESSIE. I'll tell 'er, but it won't do any good. Gawd—what a life; what with all this extra work and Nellie acting like she was goin' off 'er rocker. The old place isn't the same.

(*Takes up tray and goes off* L. CHRISTINE *sits down thoughtfully on* VIVIANNE'S *bed.* HELEN *enters* L. *She looks pale and dishevelled and quite unlike her usual self. She clutches a handkerchief in her hand and looks as if she has been crying. She is in a dressing-gown.)*

HELEN. I thought I heard your voice. Has Jessie told you? I knew you'd be upset, with Vivianne such a close friend of yours.

CHRISTINE (*rising*). She could hardly tell me anything. How is Vivianne? I want to see her.

HELEN. It wouldn't be any use, dear. She hasn't asked for anyone—only Johnny. It's doubtful whether she'll regain consciousness again.

CHRISTINE. She isn't dying?

HELEN (*sitting in chair above table*). You know that everything was against her from the start.

CHRISTINE. But why don't they take her to hospital?

HELEN (*dabbing her eyes*). I wouldn't let them. It was the one thing that she made me promise. "Whatever happens, Mrs. Allistair, whatever they say to you—don't let them take me to hospital where people will know who I am." You remember that valuable bracelet she had? She even gave me that to cover the expense if anything went wrong. Did Jess tell you how we found her? Olga called me at eleven o'clock on Monday night. She must have turned dizzy again and fallen.

CHRISTINE. Wasn't anyone at home?

HELEN. You know it was bank holiday? Molly was working, and the other girls were out. I let Sally go to bed early because she wasn't feeling very well. (*With a sigh.*) If only I'd gone down—but it never occurred to me that she wasn't safely in her bed. It's awful to think of what she must have suffered. (*More dabbing with her handkerchief. After a pause.*) Would you like to see the baby?

CHRISTINE. I want to see Viv. Surely, if she's unconscious, it can't make any difference? (*She moves L. of table.*)

HELEN. I'm only telling you what the doctor said. (*After a pause, gets another cup from the dresser and looks round for the teapot.*) I really don't know what I'm doing. After all these years, to have two tragedies following one on top of the other. I was fond of Vivianne. I wanted to look after her myself. I was trained as a nurse, you know. (*Picks up her empty cup helplessly and puts it down on table again.*) I suppose Jessie has taken the teapot upstairs?

CHRISTINE (*grimly—indicating her own cup*). You'd better have this.

HELEN (*sitting*). Thank you, my dear. I'm really not myself. I've been sitting up all night waiting for them to call me. Every time I hear a step outside my door I think she's gone.

(*With a sigh, which she breaks off as* OLGA *enters* L. *in her outdoor clothes.*)

OLGA (*cheerfully*). Hullo, Christine! Couldn't you keep away from the old homestead?

CHRISTINE. I came to see Viv. If only I'd known, I'd have come over sooner, but I suppose it couldn't have made much difference.

OLGA. What do you mean? She'll be tickled to death to see you. Does she know you're here?

CHRISTINE (*puzzled*). No, Mrs. Allistair said she wasn't conscious.

OLGA. Well she may not be awake—but she was doing fine this morning, when I looked in.

HELEN (*starting*). They let you see her?

OLGA. Sure—this morning—just before I went out. The nurse isn't a bad old stick, when you get to know her. She asked me not to let on to the others that I'd been in, in case they started barging in and out all day.

HELEN. I don't believe you.

OLGA. Nurse is ever so pleased with the way she's picking up.

(*She goes to the mantelpiece mirror and takes off her hat.*)

CHRISTINE. Did you talk to her?

OLGA. Only for a moment. She's still pretty weak and they'd given her something to make her sleep. She seemed quite bright, though.

HELEN. You're lying, Olga. You don't really expect me to believe they let you in after refusing me?

(OLGA *shrugs*.)

Nurse promised to call me as soon as she was conscious. (*Dazedly, to* CHRISTINE.) Don't listen to her. She's trying to raise your hopes for nothing. Vivianne *couldn't* get well after all she's suffered. She doesn't want to live.

OLGA. That's where you're wrong. Her one idea is to get well as soon as possible.

CHRISTINE (*to* HELEN *with disgust*). I believe you *want* her to die.

(*Breaks off as* JESSIE *enters sulkily* L., *followed by* NURSE *carrying the tea-tray.* NURSE *is a kind, brisk woman of about fifty. Her contempt for* JESSIE *is very obvious.*)

NURSE (*putting tray on table*). Can't even wash a cup up properly. Sorry, Mrs. Allistair, but I don't fancy food off crockery smeared with other people's lipstick.

HELEN. That was very careless of you, Jess.

JESSIE (R. *of table*). So what? We 'aven't got the plague.

NURSE. In a place like this, one would expect to find at least some elementary knowledge of hygiene.

JESSIE. Listen 'ere—if you're figurin' on turning the 'ouse into an 'ospital you'll 'ave to call in some more 'elp. I've 'ad enough of it. I'm not a ruddy ward maid.

HELEN (*faintly*). Everyone has to make a little extra effort in the case of emergency. Look at me. I've not complained at having the house turned upside down.

NURSE. Speaking as an outsider, I should say it looked in very much better condition than it was a couple of days ago, when I arrived.

HELEN. We're rather understaffed.

NURSE. That may be. I came down here to use your telephone
and also, if it isn't too much trouble, to ask you for a jug of
boiling water: (*To* JESSIE, *darkly.*) clean water, if you please.

HELEN (*warningly—nodding towards the kitchen*). Jess.

(*Exit* JESSIE, *grumbling.*)

CHRISTINE (*nervously*). I came to see my friend.

NURSE (*turning to her*). Are you Christine?

(*As* CHRISTINE *nods.*)

NURSE. Vivianne told me quite a lot about you. You're the
one whose husband's just got back from America, right?

HELEN (*very shaken*). You said she couldn't talk to anyone.

NURSE (*ignoring* HELEN. *To* CHRISTINE). I want to have a word
with you. Perhaps you'd like to sit with her while I prepare
her supper tray.

CHRISTINE (*relieved*). Oh, may I?

NURSE. Don't wake her, though. She's just dropped off to
sleep. That's why I took the opportunity to slip away for a
few moments. It seems she's terrified of being left alone.
(*Turns and looks steadily at* HELEN *for a moment.*) Funny thing
—a girl like that—she doesn't strike me as being the nervous
type.

HELEN (*half-rising*). I'll go and sit with her.

NURSE. I made that suggestion earlier in the day, and it took me
the best part of an hour to calm her down. If it wasn't quite
absurd, I should say she was frightened of you, Mrs. Allistair.

HELEN. Afraid of me—after all I've done for her? I couldn't
have given her better care if she'd been my own daughter.
(*With self-pity.*) It's always the way with these girls: they
haven't any sense of gratitude. Someone's only got to say a
word against me and they all follow like a lot of sheep.

(*As* JESSIE *enters—appealingly.*)

You know how fond I am of Vivianne?

JESSIE (*moving up to window*). Like hell I do.

HELEN. I haven't been to bed these last two nights in case she asked for me.

NURSE. Then I should take a couple of aspirins and go right now. I can give you my word she's entirely out of danger.

HELEN. Oh no! They all say that. I know you mean well but you can't deceive me. I've been a nurse myself.

NURSE (coldly). Believe what you like. I admit I've been a little worried about the patient's mental state, but since we've had a little talk she's been more settled in her mind: otherwise, her condition is completely satisfactory. Perhaps you'd like to confirm my report with the doctor? He should be down in half an hour. I'm hoping that a chat with him will clear up a number of the problems that have been troubling my patient.

(HELEN rises and stares at her in silent panic. The others look at her curiously. NURSE turns to CHRISTINE, who is by the fireplace.)

I rather think she'd like you to remain—you may be able to help him.

CHRISTINE. Yes—of course.

NURSE. You're the mother of the little boy who died here a few days ago?

(CHRISTINE nods.)

Forgive me for bringing up the subject—but, was his name Frankie?

CHRISTINE (distressed). No.

NURSE. Then it must have been the other child—we'll get it straightened out.

(Breaks off as MOLLY enters L., very worried.)

MOLLY. Nurse.

NURSE. What is it?

MOLLY. It's Vivianne, Nurse. You'd better come.

(HELEN sinks down in her chair, covering her face with her hands.)

(*Glancing over her shoulder.*) I tried to stop her, but she wouldn't listen.

(*They all turn towards the door* L. *as* VIVIANNE *enters very slowly and carefully. She's in her nightdress and barefooted. Her progress is unsteady and she holds on to the doorway for support.*)

NURSE (*starts towards her taking her arm*). Good heavens, are you trying to kill yourself?

VIVIANNE (*clinging to her*). I thought you'd left me.

NURSE. You silly girl, I'd only gone to get your supper. (*To* OLGA.) Help me to put her on the bed.

(*They support* VIVIANNE *to her own divan,* NURSE *at the head and* OLGA L. *of it.*)

That's right—another pillow, please.

(CHRISTINE *gets pillow from the other bed,* D.R.)

VIVIANNE (*weakly*). I thought she'd sent you away.

NURSE. What nonsense! Didn't I tell you not to worry?

(*Glances at* HELEN *who has begun to weep nervously.*)

VIVIANNE (*raising herself a little—with a faint smile*). Sorry to disappoint you.

MOLLY (*up* L.). I couldn't believe my eyes when I saw her walking down the passage.

VIVIANNE. I'm sorry, nurse—but I told you not to leave me.

NURSE. And I told you we'd got everything under control. The doctor will be here any minute: what's he going to say when he finds you down here?

(*As* VIVIANNE *begins to sob weakly—puts her arm round her.*)

There, there, dear. I'm not angry but it was a silly thing to do. As if I'd leave you after all you've told me.

HELEN (*her voice rising*). What has she been telling?

(*She makes a movement towards* VIVIANNE. CHRISTINE *crosses between her and* VIVIANNE *and sits* R. *of divan.*)

VIVIANNE. She tried to kill me, Christine: she wanted me to die.

HELEN. She's lying—lying.

VIVIANNE. I'm glad you've come. I've been wanting to tell you. (*Turning her head on the pillow restlessly.*) But I can't tell you properly now—I feel too tired. You'll have to ask Sally.

NURSE (*as* CHRISTINE *turns to her anxiously*). It's all right—she's told me all I need to know already.

VIVIANNE. When I've had a sleep you'd better call a policeman, and he can write it all down. I don't think I've forgotten anything.

JESSIE (*down* R. *of table*). What's she talking about?

HELEN. She's a lying slut.

VIVIANNE. You must ask Sal; it's Sal's little boy who's buried in the garden.

NURSE. The doctor will be here soon, and you can tell him all about it.

OLGA. I don't know what all this is about, but I should think a policeman would be more in keeping. My God, you're going to have something to answer for. Lucky for you it's not a murder charge.

HELEN ·(*centre stage, turning from one to another: they seem to have closed round her in a ring*). Sluts, all of you, with your rotten little bastards. I took you off the streets, when decent people wouldn't look at you. God, when I think what I've done for you; slaved morning and night. What have I kept for myself, since my husband died? I gave up my house to you, and this is how you repay me. You've no gratitude, no loyalty.

CHRISTINE. Get her out of here.

HELEN. Get me out of here. How dare you speak to me, you sanctimonious little bitch?

OLGA. Okay, hold your tongue; save all that for the police.

HELEN. Police. There are a few things I'd like to say to them about some of you. It's their word against mine. Nurse, what's their word against mine?

JESSIE. Nellie, do you want to put us all in quod?

HELEN (*turning on her*). You say that to me! There's nothing happened in this house that you haven't been a party to.

JESSIE. Well, something's happened now, and I'm getting out of here.

HELEN. You're staying to see this thing through with me.

JESSIE. Sorry, Nellie; you heard what they said. The police are coming. You've had your fling, and I don't suppose you'll be needing me where you're going. (*She moves towards door* L.)

HELEN. But Jessie, you've been with me for years. You've got to wait and tell them what a terrible mistake they're making.

JESSIE (*turning in doorway*). I'm not telling anybody anything. That's being a pal, isn't it? I've seen just the same as all the rest, but my memory's not as good as some; and it just so happens I'm not all that struck on policemen. (*Exit* L.)

HELEN (*screaming*). Jess, come back, you bloody fool!

(*She is now in a state of hysteria. She rushes off* L. *after* JESSIE. NURSE *and* OLGA *follow her, and we hear her screams and sobs, dying away off-stage.* MOLLY *shuts the door behind her, and then comes to head of the divan.*)

VIVIANNE (*after a long pause*). I've got to do it, Chris. I've got to make her pay—for Christopher and Sal and all of us— but I can't tell you now.

CHRISTINE (*sitting* R. *of divan*). No, darling—don't tell me anything now.

VIVIANNE. I thought it would make me feel good to see her cornered and afraid—but it didn't—it reminded me of Johnny. They won't hurt her, will they?

CHRISTINE (*soothingly*). Of course not.

VIVIANNE. Do you think she was mad?

CHRISTINE. I don't know, dear—try not to think about it.

(*There is a short pause.*)

VIVIANNE. Chris, have you seen my baby? She's beautiful!

CHRISTINE. I always thought she would be.

VIVIANNE. Would you get her for me, Molly?

(MOLLY *goes out* L. VIVIANNE *sits up a little.*)

It's a pity to think, however much I love her, I can never do her anything but harm. When this case comes up, they'll rake up all the old dirt about me and Johnny.

(*Enter* MOLLY L., *carrying the baby in a shawl; she gives it to* VIVIANNE.)

It seems awfully hard on her: I'd like her to have everything. Look at her, Chris. Isn't she the prettiest baby that you ever saw?

CHRISTINE (*after a pause—keeping her voice steady*). I believe she is ... She's all you've got, Viv.

MOLLY. She's like a little doll—and, God willing, she'll grow up a beautiful lady.

CHRISTINE (*looking at* VIVIANNE). She's very like you. (*Glances at* MOLLY *and nods towards the door.* MOLLY, *understanding, goes out* L.)

Viv. (*She rises, and stands behind* VIVIANNE. VIVIANNE *leans back; she is smiling now in spite of herself as she looks at the child*).

Viv—I hardly dare ask this—maybe it's not the proper time ...

VIVIANNE (*quickly*). Go on.

CHRISTINE. I never told you, but the doctor said I shouldn't have another baby. It didn't worry me as long as I had Christopher, but Ron and I are very fond of children. We've got a home to go back to in America and enough money to live comfortably.

VIVIANNE (*quickly—in a whisper*). Yes.

CHRISTINE. Last night we were discussing the idea of adopting a child. Ron was in favour of it, but I said just anybody's child could never be quite the same. (*After a pause.*) It wouldn't—not anybody's child—but yours, Viv—I'd love her from the start.

(Breaks off sharply as VIVIANNE *turns her face to the pillow, struggling to control her sobs.* CHRISTINE *moves round to* R. *of divan again.)*

Oh, darling, I'm sorry. I shouldn't have suggested it. Please —please don't cry, I didn't mean to upset you.

VIVIANNE *(raising herself)*. It's just what I've been praying you'd suggest. *(Sits up a little, hugging her.)* There's nothing else in the world I want so much. No—no, that wouldn't do. If you adopted her, she'd have your name. She needn't ever know she wasn't your child, need she?

CHRISTINE. Not if that's the way you want it.

VIVIANNE. It *is* the way I want it. Chris, have you considered the chance you'd be taking—knowing who her father was?

CHRISTINE. I know who her mother is, and that's why I want her.

(Returning VIVIANNE'S *hug warmly. Then as she releases herself, helps her to lie back on the pillows.)*

VIVIANNE *(after a pause)*. Will you do something for me—will you let me see you hold her?

*(*CHRISTINE *lifts the child from her. The light is fading and she stands before the window, silhouetted as in the opening of the first scene.* VIVIANNE *looks at her with a little sigh of contentment.)*

CHRISTINE *(smiling)*. All right?

VIVIANNE. All right.

She lies back hidden in the darkness, so that only CHRIS-TINE'S *silhouette is visible against the pale light of the window as*

THE CURTAIN SLOWLY FALLS

PROPERTY PLOT

Act I Scene 1

R. *of table:* suitcase (with dressing-gown).

On table: dirty crockery.

On dresser: small radio.

On clothes-horse: baby-linen, nappies, etc.

On clothes-line: stockings, blouse.

On divan L. newspaper, (under pillow) dressing-gown.

On cupboard top: sponge-bag and towel.

In cupboard drawer: small hand-mirror, jar of cold cream, removing tissues or towel.

Off-stage L. clock strike (deep note).
        small knitting-bag (LAURA).

Off-stage R. two cups of tea (CHRISTINE).
        plate and dishcloth (LAURA).

Personal: bracelet (VIVIANNE).
        apron (JESSIE).

Act I Scene 2

In fireplace: bucket and shovel.

On floor by divan L. newspapers.

Under divan pillow: dressing gown (VIVIANNE).

In vase on mantelpiece: cigarette (JESSIE).

On table: box of matches.

Off-stage L. laundry, baby-linen (HELEN).
        carrier-bag with tin of strawberries, 1 lb. of butter, packet of sweets (CHRISTINE).

Off-stage R. glass of water (CHRISTINE).
        clock strike.

Personal: potatoes, knife and bowl (SAL).
        bracelet (VIVIANNE).
        magazine (VERONICA).
        nail varnish, handbag, lipstick, etc. (OLGA).

Act II Scene 1

On table: breakfast things, loaf, jam jar, bottle of milk, toast, etc., dirty crockery.
On divan L. small, fibre trunk packed with clothes; cord, labels.
In cupboard drawer: darning silk and needle.
Off-stage L. tea-tray with tea-things (SAL).
         bath towel (CHRISTINE).
         three envelopes and one postcard (LAURA).
         clock strike.
Personal: comb, handbag with make-up, cigarettes and matches (OLGA).

Act II Scene 2

R. *of* VIVIANNE'S *divan:* small bassinet on iron stand with baby in it.
On table: small flask of brandy and glass.
         handbag (OLGA).
On back of door L. coat (OLGA), coat (VERONICA).
Off-stage L. small suitcase (CHRISTINE).
Off-stage R. baby's bottle half-full of milk (VERONICA).

Act III Scene 1

At foot of divan L. coat (VIVIANNE).
Personal: knitting in knitting-bag (MOLLY).

Act III Scene 2

On table: clean table-cloth.
On dresser: cup and saucer.
Off-stage L. tea-tray with tea-things (JESSIE).
Off-stage R. teapot, extra cup and saucer (JESSIE).
         baby in shawl (MOLLY).
Note: strike clothes-line in front of dresser after Act II.